Car Dog Millionaire

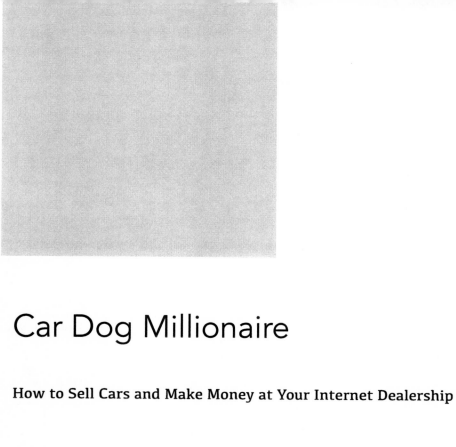

Car Dog Millionaire

How to Sell Cars and Make Money at Your Internet Dealership

Jim Flint with Michelle Lenzen

ISBN-10: 0692596437
ISBN-13: 9780692596432
Library of Congress Control Number: 2015918735

To the Car Dogs and Car Dog Millionaires:
You drive this business and deserve the credit
for taking the automotive industry to the next level.
Thanks for all your hard work.

Table of Contents

Prologue

I don't spend much time looking back. As an innovator and entrepreneur, I look forward.

To get to where we are going in this book though, you will need a few key pieces of background information. The answers to each of the following questions established my foundation and will shape our future together as you turn the pages of the book.

1. When did you get started in digital marketing?

It happened in 1983. At twelve years old, I begged my parents for an Atari 2600, the classic console game that brought us Pong, Pac-Man, and Pitfall! The 2600 was arguably the most popular gaming console of the gaming console era. You'd plug in a cartridge—just like Nintendo—and you could play any of a myriad of games via the iconic red-button joystick.

Instead of the 2600, though, my dad brought home the Atari 800 XL. It wasn't what I had in mind. It had a full keyboard, 64k of memory, *and* included the BASIC programming language.

Dad (a cryptographer in the air force, squadron commander, and Princeton graduate) and Mom (education major and schoolteacher) decided early that they would promote the learning aspects of video games. Just as we've learned that texting and driving isn't the best thing to be doing, they had an early intuition that too much time on video games wasn't a good thing.

As an ironic consequence of Dad's decision, I spent as much or more time programming visuals from the era as I did playing video games. I'd plot, chart, and colorize arrays of x and y coordinates for the MTV icon or the *Ghostbusters* logo. Hours of programming and tedious work turned into highly digitized images. By the time algebra II, geometry, and calculus arrived in high school, I had intuitive command of many of the concepts.

Then, several years later, during college, the Internet arrived. West Coast sports scores that were previously unattainable became real time. With a tip of the cap to Malcolm Gladwell and his fabulous book *Outliers: The Story of Success*, I was well down the path of the ten thousand hours it takes to become outstanding at something well before I knew it.

A few programming courses in college, an MBA with heavy emphasis in statistics, and a career of allocating resources for private distributors, retailers, and original equipment manufacturers (OEMs) provided me with a unique academic and real-world combination that affords me the opportunity to share with you some of the lifetime of experiences that I have acquired.

2. When did you get started in the car business?

In 1990, I bought my first car. It thankfully ended up being a red 1990 Mustang LX hatchback because of my younger sister, Cindy. My dad had me ready to take on an '88 Chevy Cavalier, but when my sister saw it she turned up her nose and said she'd rather take the bus to school. As a result, Dad and I went back to the dealership and came back with the Mustang. Cindy's disdain for the Cavalier ended up being a game changer.

Without the Mustang, I'd have landed in another industry. Thanks to her input, I went from having a car that struggled with sales volume and ultimately ended production in 2005 to owning one of the classic cars of our business.

When I told this story to journalist Brian Chee in an interview for DrivingSales.com, he captured some of what I think happened: "The difference between digital leaders who get it and those who pretend? It's sort of like the difference between a luxury car and a compact. The econobox will get you from A to B—sometimes—while the luxury car makes arriving at your destination a rich and valuable experience. One's a keeper. A fond memory. The other, well…some things are just best forgotten."[1]

3. With the brutal competition and relentless change, what keeps you in the space? Most people don't last. Yet here you are almost twenty years later.

My wife Cheryl is incredibly supportive. She's beautiful, smart, and kind. People who like me like me better after meeting her.

The people I work with grow and develop quickly. Whether that's dealers, suppliers, or the wonderful employees at Local Search Group, they make it worthwhile.

. . .

---

1 "DSES Speaker Profile: Jim Flint," Brian Chee, Driving Sales. Last Modified August 12, 2012, http://www.drivingsales.com/blogs/DrivingSales/2012/08/20/dses-speaker-profile-jim-flint.

And it's these elements that combine to deliver the interesting, complicated experiences that set the stage for this book.

Inspired by the 2008 movie *Slumdog Millionaire*, this book takes you on the journey of a dealer in the hot seat. In the Academy Award-winning film, a Mumbai teen from the slums becomes a contestant on *Who Wants to Be a Millionaire?* The young man gets every answer to each of the questions he's asked correct; however, he is suspected of cheating and goes through a brutal police interrogation as a result. As we learn, the correct answers to the questions came from his unique life experiences.

In the pages that follow, I share with you some of the unique life experiences that will help you answer the toughest questions leaders face in the digital marketing arena. I hope to turn you into a Car Dog Millionaire through the experiences I share. That's what I have in mind. Enjoy!

Introduction

In 2014, Amazon.com sold more than two billion items world-wide.[2] From tablets and TVs to cookbooks with Coolio and ten-foot-long garages, almost everything can be bought on Amazon—everything except cars.

Despite the Internet's ability to engulf the consumer buying experience, car sales still happen in person. While charisma and enthusiasm remain valuable in the people business of the auto-motive world, car dealers today need more than just traditional tactics to excel. They need to master the Internet, if for nothing more than survival.

The Internet's intrusion into the car industry was inevitable, if not unappreciated. The final transaction may end at the dealer-ship, but the consumer car-buying process now starts long be-fore—on the web. Though some of the best business people in the automotive category resisted as long as they possible could, digital dealerships are now reshaping the industry's thinking.

---

2 "Amazon Sellers Sold Record-Setting More Than 2 Billion Items Worldwide in 2014," Amazon.com, Business Wire. Last Modified January 5, 2015, http://www.businesswire.com/news/home/20150105005186/en/Amazon-Sellers-Sold-Record-Setting-2-Billion-Items#.VSuvV_nF8kE.

More precisely, the tipping point in the highly competitive game of selling cars is shifting to digital sales operations.

From a business perspective, car dealers and their employees conduct thousands of transactions each month at incredibly small margins. With a steady hand, they can make it all up in volume. If they seize their market opportunities and make the right choices, they can capitalize and walk away as millionaires. From the Internet clueless to the tech-savvy trailblazers, the people who use their experiences to make calculated decisions finish on top. It takes an entrepreneurial mind-set fueled by grit, gasoline, and precise knowledge to win the game. And in the dealership world, determined underdogs rise.

The key to success lies not in knowing everything but in understanding the most critical facets of marketing on the Internet. Every little decision made in your marketing strategy, advertising allocations, and digital sales operation creates a cumulative effect. It's not where you start from in the beginning; it's where you take it to by the end.

So are you ready to be a Car Dog Millionaire?

LEVELING THE PLAYING FIELD

As an advertising executive with experience working for thousands of car dealerships, I study the dynamic landscape of advertising, sales, and resource allocation. The evolution of media, consumers, and dealerships has become increasingly more sophisticated over time, and I want to help dealers take back control. I believe complexities create opportunities and throwing money at problems is not the answer. When you focus your energy strategically on the highest impact areas, you create a better path for success.

With efficiency in mind, this book addresses the most critical aspects of automotive advertising strategies and digital sales operations in the twenty-first century. I hope to capture some of the best thinking, some of the best conversations, and some of the best ways to move forward. Part One takes you on a journey through a game of "Who Wants to Be a Car Dog Millionaire," with each chapter standing alone as a guide to dissect one question dealers face in the hot seat.

In Part Two, I share some of the most interesting conversations I've had with dealers through the years. They are entertaining, honest, and filled with doubt, resistance, and confusion from dealers trying to understand the ways in which the Internet reshaped the industry.

Of course, no two dealerships are the same. Yet with a strategic approach, the core principles of marketing can be applied and adapted to identify your unique situation, market, and resources.

I share my knowledge and experiences to push the industry forward, and so you can drive your dealership ahead. Great ideas fail without the right people. No matter how digital your dealership becomes, I believe that having the right people, the right experiences, and the right knowledge matters more. Each element is intricately intertwined and helps to make up the experiences the Internet brings to the table. Whether you are an old-school Car Dog or a multimillionaire dealer principal, you can take the experiences from this book to help you turn the corner on becoming a Car Dog Millionaire. You just have to get in the game.

So let the game begin!

—Jim Flint, President and Founder of Local Search Group

Part I

Are You Ready to Be a Car Dog Millionaire?

One

How Did We Get HERE?

1. What is the moral of Aesop's fable, "The Grasshopper and the Ant?"

A. Beware of flatterers

B. Slow and steady wins the race

C. Better beans and bacon in peace than cakes and ale in fear

D. To work today is to eat tomorrow

On September 13, 2008, Hurricane Ike unleashed terror on the Texas coast—obliterating land, taking lives, and crushing infrastructure as it tore through Galveston and then Houston. With sustained winds of more than 110 miles per hour, the hurricane slammed inland with such force, it sent remnants rippling through the United States and Canada. The wicked storm dissipated two days later, leaving behind a path of destruction, immediate property damage of more than $29 billion, and estimated long-term financial damage of $142 billion.[3]

---

3 . "The Deadliest, Costliest, and Most Intense United States Tropical Storms from 1851 to 2010 (And Other Frequently Requested Hurricane Facts)," Blake, E. S., Landsea, C. W., and Gibney, E. J., Miami, Florida, NOAA Technical Memorandum

For Texas, the hurricane proved to be the costliest tropical event on record. It struck down power lines and kept the major metro market in the dark for days. In the midst of the aftermath and electrical outages, another catastrophe hit the nation.

This calamity crept in slowly before ultimately shocking the financial markets. After years of bad mortgage finance and real estate investments, hundreds of billions of dollars in losses piling up became too heavy for financial institutions to bear. On September 15, 2008, just two days removed from Hurricane Ike, Lehman Brothers collapsed in the largest bankruptcy filing in US history.[4] Holding over $600 billion in assets financed with just $30 billion in equity at the time, Lehman Brothers folded and brought down the US house of cards and a significant portion of the global market with it.[5]

Though the bankruptcy went relatively unnoticed in the days following the hurricane tragedy in areas affected by the storm, it changed the landscape of the financial markets as one faltering company after the other came crashing down. The collapse intensified the Great Recession and infiltrated businesses across the nation. With an uncertain economy, consumers lived in fear and held tightly to their wallets.

For the automotive industry, this signaled the beginning of very dark days. Sales plummeted as cars rarely moved from lots and bad days followed more bad days. On the brink of collapse,

---

NWS NHC-6. Last Modified August 2011, http://www.nhc.noaa.gov/pdf/nws-nhc-6.pdf. Also see "Effects of Hurricane Ike in Texas," Wikipedia. Last Modified October 30, 2015, https://en.wikipedia.org/wiki/Effects_of_Hurricane_Ike_in_Texas.

4 "Lehman Files for Bankruptcy; Merrill Is Sold Sorkin," A. R., Anderson, J., and Dash, E., *New York Times*. Last Modified September 14, 2008, http://www.nytimes.com/2008/09/15/business/15lehman.html?pagewanted=all.

5 "Lehman Brothers Files For Bankruptcy, Scrambles to Sell Key Business," CNBC.com. Last Modified September 15, 2008, http://www.cnbc.com/id/26708143.

the industry entered an automotive depression. During this time, demand for new automobiles went from approximately 17 million new vehicle sales per year and dropped to an annual rate of only 10 million.[6] Successful dealers went bankrupt. The situation looked grim.

Over 120,000 auto industry jobs were lost in November 2008.[7] I watched the volatile market crush job security and spare few. As uncertainty crept in, the Internet loomed even larger on the horizon: a beacon of light and hope for those who saw the possibility and a blinding, piercing sunset of ultraviolet radiation for those who chose to ignore it. Amid a backdrop of doubt, indecision, and hesitation, a new day was indeed dawning.

As a result of the financial collapse, credit markets tightened and the storm raged on. Yet the Internet kept churning through it all. And—for better or for worse—the landscape of retail automotive entered an unprecedented era as it began rebuilding and reshaping itself in the form of Internet departments that ultimately transformed into digital dealerships.

While fear of the automotive crisis still ran rampant, a glimmer of hope came with a bill called Cash for Clunkers in July 2009. If passed, this program would pay consumers up to $4,500 in credit for trading in their cars or trucks for more fuel-efficient vehicles. With a government-sponsored incentive program, I recognized the immense opportunity ahead and set out on a mission. If I could master the Internet today, we could be victorious tomorrow.

---

6 "If Detroit Falls, Foreign Makers Could Be Buffer," Uchitelle, L., *New York Times.* Last Modified November 16, 2008, http://www.nytimes.com/2008/11/17/business/economy/17impact.html?_r=2&hp&oref=slogin&.

7 "The Resurgence of the American," The White House. Last Modified June 2011, https://www.whitehouse.gov/sites/default/files/uploads/auto_report_06_01_11.pdf.

In the second quarter of 2009, I worked to build a Cash for Clunkers website based off the legislation. I included every car from every manufacturer and the estimated miles per gallon for each car. No one knew if the bill would pass, but I tailored the website to be a trusted resource just in case it did.

On August 7, 2009, the bill passed.[8] I woke up elated, knowing everyone everywhere searching online would find my website. I jumped on the computer for a triumphant Google Search. Unfortunately, what came back reshaped my thinking: sponsored ad…sponsored ad…sponsored ad.

My brief elation quickly shifted to frustration. Though my SEO-ranked website was number one in Texas, it showed up as the fourth site down the line. SEM was trumping my work. Major automotive groups like Sonic and Van Tuyl had purchased the right keywords and commandeered the top three slots above my website. In disbelief, I clicked on the links of the sponsored ads and each one brought me to a dealership's website with no information about the program. No miles per gallon estimates, no way to contact the dealer. Nothing.

After two months of work, getting out-executed at the finish line wasn't a good feeling. Notably a few other SEO-oriented websites existed, and they too were chock-full of great information—including one from the government and one from Brian Pasch and his team. However, I had missed the search engine marketing opportunity. As such I called my pay per click account director on Friday morning and asked her to put together a pay per click campaign. She noted that it might take a few days to get everything built out. Sensing her company's lack of urgency,

---

8 "Cash for Clunkers Extension Signed into Law," Liberto, J., *CNN Money*. Last Modified August 7, 2009, http://money.cnn.com/2009/08/07/autos/clunkers_continu es/?postversion=2009080711.

I took the reins and spent $500 of my own money to create my first Google AdWords campaign on Saturday morning. With time, relevancy, and the market on our side, I knew I needed to seize this opportunity fast. We couldn't wait for delays from our marketing agency.

By the next day, the online traffic had exhausted my $500. On average, people spent seven minutes on the site and looked at more than seven pages—remarkably great statistics.

Next, I added another major metro market and upped the ante to $1,000. I shared the results with my dealership group, who gave me the green light to keep going. On a roll, I spent another $5,000 advertising the Cash for Clunkers program. Investing in Google Ads proved to be a catalyst for business. In the weeks that followed, we gained over five hundred e-mail subscribers and more than a hundred leads, which ended in nearly twenty-five car sales.

Though I couldn't control the Google algorithm, I could advertise the words I wanted, when I wanted, in the places I wanted. Getting my dealership group in front of people at the right time proved profitable for business. In times of need, people click on relevant information.

Despite the tough times of economic turmoil, the future looked bright.

CHAPTER 1 SUMMARY

Answer: D, to work today is to eat tomorrow.

Key Point: Like the industrious ant, it is best to prepare for the days of necessity. Forward thinkers make the best marketers; mastering online advertising today distinguishes Car Dogs from Car Dog Millionaires.

Summary:

- Both environmental and economic catastrophes struck the nation in 2008 and amplified the Great Recession.
- During the automotive industry crisis, the government's Cash for Clunkers program stimulated the economy and consumer spending on new vehicles.
- Putting an informative website in front of consumers proved to be a valuable tool in selling cars. In times of need, people search for and click on relevant information.
- To out-execute competitors online, dealers will find that Google AdWords is a powerful tool.

<u>Updates</u>

If you like the style and tone of this book, we can send you e-mail updates with our best thinking. Simply send an e-mail to jim@ localsearchgroup.com and put "Local Search Group Insights" in the subject line. Include your first name, last name, your title, and where your company is located and we'll add you to our growing list!

Two

Run the Floor with
Tiers 1, 2, and 3

2. Which of the following ABA teams did not make it into the 1976 NBA merger?

A. San Antonio Spurs

B. Denver Nuggets

C. Saint Louis Spirits

D. Indiana Pacers

When the American Basketball Association (ABA) and the National Basketball Association (NBA) merged in 1976, the NBA only accepted four of the seven ABA teams and planned to dismantle the remaining three: the Virginia Squires, Kentucky Colonels, and Saint Louis Spirits.[9] Though the Squires went bankrupt before the merger, the owners from the other two teams negotiated compensation deals. While Kentucky Colonels owner John Y. Brown accepted a $3.3 million payout, Saint Louis Spirit owners Daniel and Ozzie Silna locked down a deal that would make them an estimated $300 million by 2014.[10]

---

9 "1976 NBA Merges with ABA," History.com. Last Modified (n.d.). Accessed September 4, 2015, http://www.history.com/this-day-in-history/nba-merges-with-aba.

10 "Deal of a Lifetime: Brothers Dunk Huge NBA Dollars without Team," Briggs, B., NBC News. Last Modified February 18, 2014, http://www.nbcnews.com/business/business-news/deal-lifetime-brothers-dunk-huge-nba-dollars-without-team-n4536.

In what is now known as one of the greatest sport deals of all time, the NBA agreed to pay the Silna brothers for any Spirit players drafted by the NBA teams along with a one-seventh share of each of the four ABA teams' NBA television rights for *eternity*.[11] Daniel and Ozzie Silna hoped this deal would allow them to eventually fulfill their dream of owning an NBA team, when and if the league expanded again. As for the NBA, the pact ended up costing them much more than they bargained for, as pro basketball's popularity exploded in the years to follow. Once Michael Jordan, Larry Bird, and Magic Johnson stepped onto the court in the 1980s and 1990s, the NBA became a global spectacle as viewers around the world tuned in to watch the games.

Almost forty years after the agreement, the NBA finally bought out the Silna brothers' deal by paying them an additional $500 million.[12] The brothers accepted the deal in large part because the money was right. However, the NBA stood poised and prepared to position the lucrative Internet rights to NBA broadcasts as *not* part of the television rights agreement that had previously been established.

Though the brothers never owned an NBA team, they taught the league a valuable lesson: if you negotiate before fully considering the outcome, you could pay a disproportionate price.

MONEY ALLOCATION AND MARKETING TIERS

As a car dealer, think about your dealership like the NBA. You need to allocate your marketing budget to the right places, and if you don't examine the environment first, you could end up

---

11 "The NBA Finally Puts an End to the Greatest Sports Deal of All Time," Burke, M., *Forbes.* Last Modified January 7, 2014, http://www.forbes.com/sites/monteburke/2014/01/07/the-nba-finally-puts-an-end-to-the-greatest-sports-deal-of-all-time/.
12 Ibid.

paying a disproportionate amount toward areas that will not provide a return on investment. To spend your ad dollars the best way you can, take the time to analyze the three most influential parts of the car selling game: the automotive marketing tiers. Tiers 1, 2, and 3 ultimately work together to sell cars, yet each one plays a different role in the process. When looked at in consecutive order, the complementary goals of each group become clear:

Tier	Group	Goal
1	National Auto Manufacturers	Buy This Brand!
2	Regional Dealer Associations	Buy Now!
3	Local Auto Dealerships	Buy Here!

Before you begin Tier 3 advertising to drive traffic to your dealership, consider all of the mediums and messaging Tiers 1 and 2 plan to use in your market. Knowing how much advertising coverage the cars on your lot will be receiving from your national and regional offices will guide you in determining where your local dealership's ad money and resources can best be allocated.

TIER 1: BUY THIS BRAND!
The golden route to Car Dog Millionaire success at the Tier 1 level starts with the manufacturers' media plan. Navigating the numbers here will show you where your dealership ranks and give you clear data points on your current standing in the national market. To begin decoding this, pull up your manufacturer's regional media plan and complete the following steps.

AUTO DEALERSHIP
MEDIA FLOWCHART

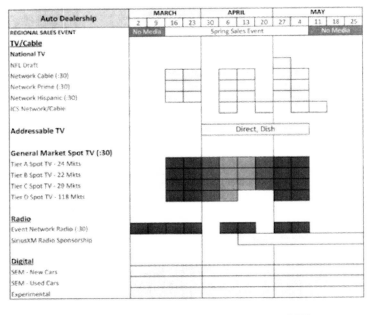

STEP 1: DETERMINE WHAT MARKET YOU ARE IN

Manufacturers use a tier system to define categories in their media plans. Notice the above spreadsheet has Tiers A, B, C, and D. You absolutely need to figure out which tier your dealership falls in. Think about it like finding out whether or not you made the varsity football team. It's a huge deal. Either you made it into a tier that the manufacturer plans to allocate hundreds of thousands of dollars to, or they could be cutting you out of the cash and putting you on the bench.

A manufacturer's tier system will categorize markets either by the amount of media they are buying or the product they are supporting. For example, Tier A could represent the markets in which they plan to spend $500,000, or it could simply represent a product like the Toyota Camry.

> JIM: *Confused about your manufacturer's spreadsheet?*
> *Give your factory representative a call!*

Your goal here is to figure out where you are on the manufacturer's radar. They may be focusing resources in your region and have a great presence in your market—giving you more brand exposure to the cars you are trying to sell. Or on the other hand, they may not be giving you any coverage, which means you will need to do a lot of heavy lifting to stay competitive and market your own dealership.

STEP 2: DECIDE TO COMPLEMENT OR SUPPLEMENT THE MEDIA PLAN

Once you figure out what tier you are in, take a look at the manufacturer's plan for the upcoming months. At this point you will need to decide if you want to complement or supplement their media plan.

- **When to Complement:** Looking at the spreadsheet, you notice there is no scheduled media coverage for Memorial Day weekend. You want to stay competitive during the holiday weekend, so you decide to buy local advertising. You complement the manufacturer's plan by working around the open areas and buying what they do not cover.

- **When to Supplement:** At the end of April, you see your manufacturer bought SiriusXM radio advertising. Knowing consumers will have more disposable income as paychecks come in at the end of the month, you want to increase your dealership exposure during this crucial buying time. You decide to buy local radio at the end of April to supplement the manufacturer's efforts on SiriusXM radio.

TIER 2: BUY NOW!

After decoding your manufacturer's media schedule, the next step involves looking to the association for sales messaging. At this level, the association allocates resources for either brand messaging or retail messaging. But which one is the most successful? Let's find out.

Say you are at a cocktail party and you meet a handful of new people. Will you remember everyone's first and last name? Probably not. Statistically speaking, the odds are you won't remember either, much less one of the two.

To find out if the same concept held true in the automotive industry, I worked with my good friends at the Nielsen Company to test my hypothesis to see if people really remembered the brand and product names in the automotive category after seeing an advertisement. Through online consumer surveys, we found across the board that people do *not* differentiate between branding and product on a consistent basis. After viewing a Toyota Camry commercial, only 21 percent of the people accurately remembered the make and model of the product.

If a regional association creates a memorable commercial in terms of story line but no one remembers the car, then Tier

2 fails to achieve its goal. The goal of Tier 2 isn't to go viral; Tier 2's messaging should create a sense of urgency for car shoppers to "buy now" with retail messaging in these three categories:

1. Lease Price Point
2. Customer Cash
3. APR Offer

Consumers shop for deals, and by giving them good deals at the right time, dealers will absolutely sell more cars. While Tier 2 messages are typically the most effective on TV and radio, digital advertising with hypermobile targeting is arguably the most efficient medium on a local level today. Stay involved with your dealers association's "buy now" messaging to better align your Tier 3 efforts.

TIER 3: BUY HERE!

Once you figure out the automotive ecosystem on a national and regional level, the only thing you have left to do is give people a reason to visit your dealership. You need to differentiate your store from the competition, especially if there are other franchisees in your DMA (designated market area).

So what drives people to the lot and motivates them to buy? From my experience working with Tier 1, Tier 2, and Tier 3 over the years, the most successful stores typically use a few age-old tactics to thrive on a Tier 3 level:

- They identify their current relationship with the market through frequent audits: "How did you hear about us?"

- They know how to use TV/radio mediums to achieve the highest ROI. It's not about volume of spots, it's about reach and frequency.
- They focus on retail over brand messaging: "Bring the sales message."

To adapt to the changing market, the dealers with the highest car sales and customer satisfaction are also setting themselves apart online. The most profitable stores I work with today are gaining a competitive edge by using the Internet in distinct and strategic ways:

- They build websites that refine their image and offer valuable information.
- They make themselves visible online with search engine optimized (SEO) content.
- They connect with and find ways to be responsive to consumers via social media.

Now more than ever, investing resources in the Internet is becoming vital for dealers to excel at Tier 3 marketing. To strengthen your dealership's online presence, sit tight in the hot seat. There will be more on that in the chapters to follow.

CHAPTER 2 SUMMARY

Answer: C, St. Louis Spirits

Key Point: Whether it's officials running the NBA or dealers running their car business, people pushing to the next level of success must navigate through obstacles to maximize their return and minimize their losses. Dealers need to figure out where their manufactures and dealer associations are putting their money to decide how to market their dealership locally. Today, Internet mastery on the Tier 3 level separates Car Dogs from Car Dog Millionaires.

Summary: To understand how all three tiers of automotive marketing work together, analyze each tier individually.

- For Tier 1, examine your manufacturer's current media plan.
  - Determine the market your dealership is grouped with.
  - Decide whether to complement or supplement Tier 1 marketing efforts:
    - Complement by buying ad slots for days the manufacturer did not cover.
    - Supplement by buying additional ad slots to make big days or weekends bigger.
- For Tier 2, work with your dealers association to create retail campaigns that instill a sense of urgency for customers to "buy now."
  - Feature deals on lease price point, customer cash, and APR.
- For Tier 3, bring consumers to your dealership with SEO, SEM, and social via the Internet.

Three

Track Your Moneyball Factor, Not Leads

3. Charles Darwin believed that evolution occurred:

    A. in quick, random bursts of new species
    B. gradually as variations were retained through successive generations
    C. only in mammals
    D. gradually after all the weak members of populations were eliminated

In 2002, the Oakland Athletics baseball team paid $41 million in salaries and somehow stayed competitive with the big dog New York Yankees, who spent well over $125 million in payroll.[13] Intrigued by this phenomenon, financial journalist Michael Lewis set out to research the Oakland A's. He met with the team's general manager Billy Beane and discovered a radically different approach to the age-old game, one that forever altered the value of statistics and for that matter Home Runs.

---

13   Lewis, M., *Moneyball: The Art of Winning an Unfair Game* (New York: W. W. Norton & Company, 2003).

While top teams used big budgets to assemble elite squads of home run hitters, the Oakland Athletics' roster featured a bunch of seemingly average guys by conventional MLB standards. Beane operated on a basic principle: teams that score runs win games. Instead of investing in players that baseball insiders deemed valuable—based on home runs, runs batted in, and batting averages—Beane invested in players who got on base. Through rigorous statistical analysis, he found on-base percentage to be the most highly correlated indicator of offensive success.

Since these traits were undervalued by the professional baseball world in the early 2000s and overshadowed by players with power, the Oakland A's compiled a team of players from the proletariat with precisely the right talent. Beane and Paul DePodesta, a Harvard graduate with a degree in economics, conducted a careful evaluation of statistics that proved successful and led to the game-winning strategies that carried the team to the playoffs in 2002 and 2003.

When Lewis shared Beane's evidence-based approach in the book *Moneyball: The Art of Winning an Unfair Game*, it rocked the baseball world and shook up business paradigms. An analytical eye on data proved stronger than the traditional wisdom trusted by the masses.

THE MONEYBALL FACTOR

I read Michael Lewis's book in 2003. Then, I read it again. General manager Billy Beane's attention to detail and DePodesta's tedious focus on decoding metrics fascinated me. The findings played over and over again in my mind years later as I sifted through my own data. Overseeing ten stores as the director of interactive sales and marketing—much akin to an e-commerce director position—my dealerships were all asking the same question: "How much money should I spend on advertising?"

It's quite a simple question for something historically uncertain. As John Wannamaker said in the early 1900s, "Half the money I spend on advertising is wasted; the trouble is, I don't know which half."

Instead of accepting that uncertainty as fate, I set forth on finding a statistically significant answer. Like Beane, I knew throwing money into the game didn't necessarily translate into making more money or guarantee success. Yet so many factors went into selling cars. From leads, trade shows, and traditional advertising on TV and radio, to the digital campaigns of the future and print campaigns of the past, marketing channels scattered broad across verticals with uncertain impact.

I wanted to find precisely the right places dealers could spend their money to maximize their earnings. With a clear mission, I commenced my comprehensive data dive for the Moneyball Factor of selling cars.

As I sat in a pit of marketing statistics, I filtered through spreadsheet after spreadsheet. I knew the golden nuggets—positive correlations between advertising budget allocation and business profit—were embedded somewhere.

I thought back to the basic premise of Beane's strategy: *Teams that score runs win games.* Using the same logic, I redefined my search: *Dealerships that sell cars make money.* Now I just needed to figure out what factor most highly correlated with selling cars. The answer seemed obvious—leads.

Since the introduction of automotive dealerships, the nature of selling cars relied heavily on the relationship side of business.

From meeting people at town fairs or at the chamber of commerce, to conversing with foot traffic, leads were one of the most trusted indicators for car sales.

I crunched the numbers for my dealerships to find out how strong of a correlation still existed between leads and sales. What I discovered surprised and perplexed me. In many cases, leads were going down as sales went up. When I traced this peculiar phenomenon back to the dealership teams, I quickly found a classic case of human manipulation. With goals and bonuses tied to closing ratios, employees were spinning leads in favor of their pay plans. Let me explain.

If a dealer pays his Internet director a $1,000 bonus for a 10 percent closing ratio, the Internet director can deliberately enter solid leads and omit soft leads to meet the quota. For example, if the employee goes to a state fair and gets contact information for unlikely car buyers, he may not enter them into the system as leads. To err on the side of financial safety, the employee manipulates his numbers to keep leads artificially low and ensure he meets the 10 percent bonus.

We also know that almost everything in the customer relationship management (CRM) systems at stores can be manipulated. As a result, the tracking mechanisms captured an inaccurate picture at best. The referral, appointment, leads, and shows didn't predict revenue as successfully as they should have. Like Beane and DePodesta, I discovered that the most reliable metrics of the past proved invaluable in the context of the present. I knew dealership dynamics were changing, and I needed to understand why.

I started again, this time taking a different approach by looking for statistically significant correlations between dealer actions and car sales. Instead of looking at the back-end numbers, I refocused on the front end with the purchase funnel. If I could grasp why consumers buy, I could figure out how to sell more and more efficiently.

In a traditional automotive purchase funnel, consumers became aware of a brand during their first interaction: *i.e.,* seeing a TV commercial for a car at a local dealership. If in the market for a new car, shoppers started considering the brand and perhaps began asking for opinions from others who had ownership experience. These interactions shaped perceptions and presumably led to an intent to purchase. Serious car shoppers then looked around at different dealerships and went for some test drives. If they liked a car more than the alternatives, they moved forward and began the purchase process.

With this simple and classic model, a greater awareness at the top of the funnel resulted in more car sales at the bottom of the funnel. Yet like old MLB performance stats, I knew innately that flaws existed in this funnel because spending more money for awareness didn't necessarily yield more car sales. With leads no longer serving as the home run hitters, the car selling process was evolving in new and different ways.

To understand why, I walked through the steps a consumer now takes to buy a car. They pull up Google…and there it was. Staring at me. The massive external force changing the game. Though it crept into the automotive industry slowly because of a resistance to change, the Internet was enabling a fundamental paradigm shift in consumerism. Instead of consuming products like our ancestors did during the industrial era, customers today consume information. Thanks to the Internet, the buying path now looks more like an hourglass than a funnel.

Once online, consumers encounter a multitude of brand interactions that simultaneously capture their awareness, shape their opinions, and sway purchase decisions. To position themselves competitively in today's market, dealerships need to stand out online to push interested buyers through the funnel and then into their physical store locations.

Echoing this theory, Google's 2015 "Auto Shopper Insights" report revealed that car buyers today visit only 1.6 dealerships before buying—a dramatically plummeting number that was closer to five dealerships just ten years ago.[14] As I read through Google's data, I realized just how much the car-buying game is changing. Today, vehicle shoppers are now researching almost exclusively online.

14 Auto Shopper Insights for 2015 Planning," Google, YouTube, Milward Brown Digital, and R.L. Polk. (2015).

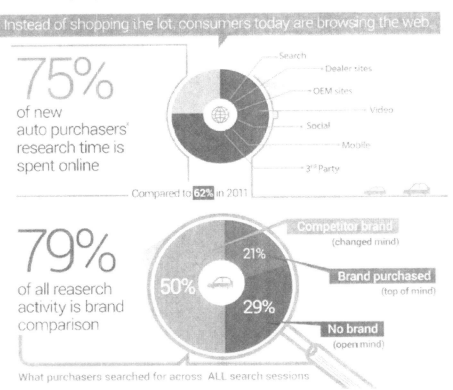

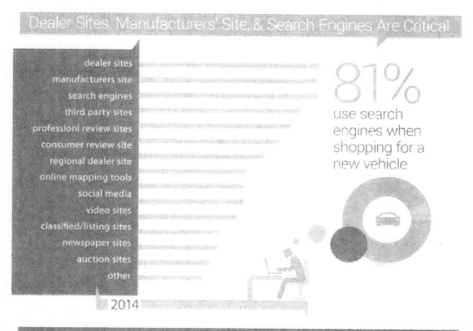

Dealer Sites, Manufacturers' Site, & Search Engines Are Critical

dealer sites
manufacturers site
search engines
third party sites
professionl review sites
consumer review site
regional dealer site
online mapping tools
social media
video sites
classified/listing sites
newspaper sites
auction sites
other

2014

81%
use search
engines when
shopping for a
new vehicle

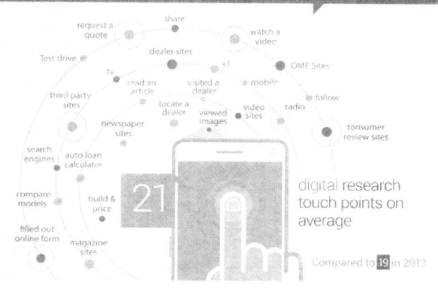

Every interaction online and offline affects purchase decisions.

request a quote
share
watch a video
Test drive
dealer sites
OME Sites
tv
+1
read an article
visited a dealer
mobile
third party sites
follow
locate a dealer
video sites
radio
viewed images
newspaper sites
tonsumer review sites
search engines
auto loan calculator
compare models
build & price
filled out online form
magazine sites

21

digital research
touch points on
average

Compared to 19 in 2013

25

Seeing all signs pointing to the power of the Internet, I went back to the analytics on my dealers' websites. I felt my thought process getting warmer and wanted to see what numbers could conclusively tie the Internet to car sales. Across the board, website traffic had increased significantly for these dealerships over time. For one client, the numbers grew from 10,000 monthly visitors in 2010 to over 30,000 in 2014.

To avoid the gamesmanship of the CRM, I narrowed my thinking down to two telling metrics I knew to be true: Google Analytic stats on website traffic and the number of cars sold as printed on the financial statement. General managers and Internet directors stopped arguing and started listening as I devised a ratio for these metrics, and for the first time, I uncovered a highly correlated indicator that was also predictive of profitability.

Moneyball Factor = # of cars sold ÷ # of unique website visitors

I ran the ratio of my Moneyball Factor for each dealership and presented my findings. More rigorous research revealed a delicate balance the maximized profitability:

Moneyball Factor	ROI	Diagnosis
< 2	Low	Overadvertising; web traffic not converting to car sales
= 2	High	Optimal advertising; web traffic positively correlating to car sales
> 2	Low	Underadvertising; focusing on operational aspects and missing business opportunities

When I conveyed the numbers and importance of the Moneyball Factor, some dealers met me with apprehension. For car guys who thrived in an era where newspapers were the key to success, throwing money at the Internet seemed foreign and uncertain. Yet few could argue with the stats. Dividing car sales by unique website visitors created an accurate ratio that could guide strategic planning and dramatically drive business performance. The data pushed general managers and Internet directors onto the same page as it shed light on an important shift in the automotive industry. To sell cars, dealers needed to adapt with technology to run Internet dealerships.

CHAPTER 3 SUMMARY

Answer: B, Charles Darwin believed evolution occurred gradually as variations were retained through successive generations.

Key Point: The automotive industry is changing. Car Dogs who want to thrive establish themselves as Internet dealerships by correlating car sales and web traffic to maximized profitability.

Summary:

- Michael Lewis's book *Moneyball* altered the way people use statistics in baseball and business.
- Just as Beane discovered that home runs were no longer the most telling stat for baseball talent, I realized leads were no longer the most reliable numbers for dealers to build their business on.
    - The Internet reshaped the traditional marketing funnel we once knew, as consumers are now cross-shopping online for new vehicles and visiting dealership websites as opposed to their physical locations. Welcome to the hourglass-shaped funnel.
- Instead of leads, the new ratio for car dealers to use is: Moneyball Factor = # of cars sold ÷ # of website visits.
- This Moneyball Factor can be used as a diagnostic tool for how effective the dealership's digital strategy is in terms of selling cars. If the Moneyball Factor is…
    - Under 2, the dealership is overadvertising and the web traffic is not converting to car sales.
    - Around 2, the dealership's online advertising is optimal.
    - Above 2, the dealership is underadvertising and leaving money on the table.

Four

Be a High Roller: Go All in on Data and Count Cars

4. MIT professor Edward O. Thorp published a book titled *Beat the Dealer* after creating a computer program to calculate all mathematical probabilities in what game?

A. Craps   B. Roulette
C. Blackjack   D. Baccarat

In 2013, Ben Affleck starred as an online poker boss in the gambling thriller *Runner Runner.* Though the movie received less-than-stellar reviews, Affleck nailed his performance. And as it turns out, it wasn't all acting.

One year later, in May of 2014, security swarmed Affleck at a high roller's blackjack table in the Hard Rock Hotel & Casino in Las Vegas and deemed him "an advantaged player"—someone too good at the game. Their cameras caught him counting cards, and the casino wanted none of that.

"I took some time to learn the game and became a decent blackjack player. And once I became decent, the casinos asked me not to play blackjack. I mean, the fact that being good at the game is against the rules at the casinos should tell you something about casinos," Affleck said after the incident in an interview with *Details Magazine*.[15]

Luckily for Affleck, his blackjack mastery started long before security intervened. Back in 2001, he reportedly won $800,000 in blackjack at the same Hard Rock casino.[16] As a proven card shark, Affleck and longtime buddy Matt Damon even competed in several World Series of Poker events together.

"I knew with blackjack that there's a way you can improve your odds. And so I started trying to learn. And then I just got to a point in my life where I'm like, 'If I'm going to do something, I'm going to try and do it really well,'" Affleck said in his interview. He realized early on that if he got good enough at the game, he could change the outcome to walk away as a millionaire. Until, of course, security intervened.

GETTING THE ODDS IN YOUR FAVOR

Becoming a millionaire in business is a lot like blackjack, only instead of counting cards, you must count data. Every company starts with a different hand, depending on their location, market, and opportunities. By analyzing time and resource allocations with direct outcomes, companies can figure out what is working, what isn't, and how they can strategically move forward to change the odds in their favor.

JIM: *If it is not worth tracking, it is not worth doing.*

---

15 "Ben Affleck—the Director's Cut," Gordinier, J., *Details*. Last Modified October 2014, http://www.details.com/culture-trends/celebrities/201410/ben-affleck-david-fincher-gone-girl?currentPage=3

16 "Ben Affleck Booted from Hard Rock Blackjack Tables for Counting Cards," Beckett, S., Casino.org. Last Modified May 6, 2014, http://www.casino.org/news/ben-affleck-booted-hard-rock-blackjack-tables-counting-cards

With the amount of data and statistical analysis tools available, choosing not to track is like leaving money on the table. Why would you keep marketing and sales a mystery when the answers lie in counting the numbers?

As the Internet continues to change the way cars are sold, the old success metrics dealers used to rely on need to be adapted. Here are the four most valuable goals dealerships should now be setting and tracking, with the Moneyball Factor from the previous chapter topping the list:

1. The Moneyball Factor

Old goal: Leads are the most highly correlated metric to a dealership's car sales.

New goal: A statistically significant relationship exists between website visitors and car sales. Instead of leads, it is this ratio—the Moneyball Factor—that is now the most highly correlated to vehicle sales. Strive for a Moneyball Factor around 2.0 to achieve the highest return on investment for your dealership.

Formula: Number of cars sold ÷ Number of unique website visitors = Moneyball Factor

2. Lead Ratios

Old goal: Get as many leads as possible.

New goal: For all the leads that come in, strive to turn 25 percent of them into appointments and have 75 percent of those appointments show up.

Chapter 4

Formulas: Total Appointments Made ÷ Total Leads = Appointment Ratio
Total Dealership Visits ÷ Total Appointments Made = Visit Ratio

While leads no longer serve as the most predictable metric for profitability, they are still valuable in gauging consumer interest and getting people into your dealership. To better understand lead ratios, let's walk through how to use them at your dealership. Say you receive 1,000 leads. With the new goal in mind, you want 25 percent of these people to make an appointment: *1,000 leads x 25 percent = 250 people*

Remember, shoppers today only visit one to two dealerships on average before buying, so securing appointments holds significant potential in maximizing your car sales. Of those 250 people who made appointments, you want to ensure that 75 percent of them show up: *250 people x 75 percent = 187 people*

So out of 1,000 initial leads, 187 appointed people should be walking into your dealership.

3. Closing Ratio

Old goal: In 2010, just five years ago, a 10 percent closing ratio was the industry benchmark.

New Goal: Today with car shoppers visiting only 1.6 dealerships on average before buying, a 10 percent closing ratio is no longer acceptable. A 25 to 30 percent closing ratio should be the minimum goal your team sets to achieve.

Formula: Total Closed Deals ÷ Total Sales Leads= Closing Ratio

Once someone walks through your doors, you have remarkably higher odds at closing the deal than five years ago. These shoppers most likely researched online and know exactly what they want. Only if you somehow spoil the deal will they head to another dealership to buy the car. Hold your team accountable by raising the bar with higher closing ratio goals.

4. Cost Per Sale

Old goal: The lower the cost per sale, the better.

New goal: Determine your current cost per sale by adding up your entire ad spend and dividing by all sales during a fixed date range. Your new strategic cost per sale ratio will be spending at or below this level.

Formula: Total Ad Expenses ÷ Total Number of Sales = Updated Cost per Sale Ratio

Dealerships with the lowest cost per sale are not necessarily the most successful. Every dealership's cost per sale varies depending on the local market and economy; one dealership's cost per sale in New York may be significantly higher than another's in Minnesota. The importance of this metric lies not in competing with other dealerships but in using it as a benchmark to compete with yourself.

A Case Study on Cost per Sale
Chris Morrison of Honda Cars of Katy set out to analyze the effectiveness of his dealership's Facebook campaigns. For

a businessman who started running his dealership thirty years ago, using the Internet seemed like a pretty foreign place to spend money in hopes of selling cars. In April 2013, Morrison's dealership spent $500 on a Facebook ad campaign that targeted two major medical centers in the Houston area. The campaign sent ads to all employees at the hospitals who had Facebook pages and led to nine vehicle sales at the dealership.

While nine cars seemed like a tiny fraction of the 311 they sold that month, the return on investment numbers told a very different story:

Cost per sale= $500 ÷ 9 vehicles= $55.56/vehicle

In traditional advertising on the radio, Morrison's dealership cost per sale had hovered around $300 per vehicle. Recognizing this advantageous return on Facebook with ads at a cost of $55.56 per vehicle sale, Honda Cars of Katy expanded their Facebook campaigns. Today, they continue to track data and measure their success by looking at cost per sale based on ad spend and vehicle sales.[17]

By intimately knowing and understanding how to adapt all four of these ratios to the current market, dealers can consistently set and measure attainable goals. Individually, employees should be using their strengths to pursue initiatives and projects that contribute to the updated goals. Collectively, the company should be holding their teams accountable for tracking tasks and measuring

---

17 "Dealer Swaps Shoe Leather for Facebook," Barkholz, D., Automotive News. Last Modified May 20, 2013, http://www.autonews.com/article/20130520/RETAIL07/305209956/dealer-swaps-shoe-leather-for-facebook.

progress toward reaching the targeted ratios. These numbers should be closely monitored and consistently redefined as time goes on with an eye toward continuously improving. Building a successful business is no longer a game of chance; it is a deliberate, metric-focused, and metric-driven opportunity.

CHAPTER 4 SUMMARY

Answer: C, Blackjack

Key Point: MIT professor Edward O. Thorp's book, *Beat the Dealer*, mathematically proved that blackjack players could overcome the house advantage with card counting. Car dealers can master their market and increase their profitability by counting data like cunning blackjack players count cards.

Summary:

- Ben Affleck played a gambling boss on screen. Off screen, he won hundreds of thousands of dollars by mastering the skill of counting cards in blackjack.
- To become a millionaire in business, you need to track data beyond the financial statement.
- If it's not worth tracking, it's not worth doing.
- Car dealers must set new goals for the following metrics and intimately understand their business's position in achieving them:
  - Moneyball Factor
    - Strive for a Moneyball Factor around 2.0 to achieve the highest return on investment for your dealership.
  - Lead Ratios
    - For all the leads that come in, turn 25 percent of them into appointments and 75 percent of those appointments into dealership visits.
  - Closing Ratio
    - Set at least a 25 to 30 percent closing ratio goal.

- Cost per Sale
  - Add up all ad spend and divide by all sales during a fixed date range. Make the goal to spend at or below this level depending on the seasonality of the business as determined by the month of the year and the number of selling weekends.

Five

Own the Game with a Strong Internet Sales Manager

5. The enemies in which game were inspired by the swine flu epidemic?

A. Angry Birds

B. Assassin's Creed

C. Hog Hunter

D. Mass Effect

G ames define generations. Aside from reflecting the evolution of technology, games also mirror current events and mindsets. They build childhood memories and become an integral part of youth. As we recall old games with nostalgia and greet new games with awe, we reflect on how the times and problem-solving strategies have changed.

In 1972, Atari launched the first ever arcade sports video game Pong.[18] The simulated table tennis game had two-dimensional graphics and a simple player objective: return the serve. The simplicity of it all—the controls, the screen, the visuals—showcased technology of the 1970s and the baby

---

18 "Pong," The International Arcade Museum. Last Modified (n.d.). Retrieved September 28, 2015, http://www.arcade-museum.com/game_detail.php?game_id=9074.

boomer mind-set: communicate clearly and always, but always, return the serve.

As time passed and technology advanced, Mario Bros. came along more than a decade later and captivated Generation Xers.[19] Players needed to help plumber brothers Mario and Luigi defeat creatures coming from the sewers in New York City. In each level, players faced systematic challenges and used trial and error to learn how to earn extra lives and overcome enemies and fireballs. With enough practice, players could memorize the series of steps needed to beat each level. Through formulated sequences, Generation Xers found comfort and success.

Next up came Generation Y, wherein Angry Birds swooped in upon the millennial masses. While making the game in 2009, the developers took note of the swine flu epidemic in the media and decided to make all the villains pigs.[20] To play the game, the contenders catapulted a bird wildly into the air through tight spaces with the primary objective to eliminate the pigs. Despite the simple concept, the game brought to light all kinds of chaos as the birds hit various obstacles along the way to uncertain outcomes. When a player finally got all the pigs, they usually didn't know how to replicate the exact path again. The thrill of the game revolved around the uncertainty and luck in it all, not in the control that a prior generation had learned. Generation Y players recognized the changing dynamic and took exciting risks to figure things out.

---

19 "Mario Bros.," StrategyWiki. Last Modified January 8, 2014, http://strategywiki. org/wiki/Mario_Bros.

20 "Bad Piggies." Angry Birds Wiki. Last Modified (n.d.). Retrieved September 28, 2015, http://angrybirds.wikia.com/wiki/Bad_Piggies.

Today, a game of a different kind in a new category is captivating Generation Z: Snapchat. With the rush of instant gratification and intimate secrecy, the Snapchat app is gamifying social sharing. Gen Zers marvel at creating stories with expiration dates that occur immediately upon consumption while simultaneously experiencing in-the-moment thrills and candid sharing within their networks.

HOW GAMES AFFECT DEALERSHIPS

With the constant evolution of games and problem-solving strategies, it's no wonder that a digital divide exists within the mix of baby boomers, Gen X, Gen Y, and Gen Z in the workforce. Individually, they all use their learned behaviors to accomplish the tasks at hand. As a team they may work together to maximize outcomes; however, the strongest leaders intuitively know the metrics of their own game and seek to understand the games and mind-sets of the different generations.

To catapult your store and to make the changes necessary to become an Internet dealership, dealerships must find a balance between the older generations that thrive on control and younger generations that take risks in tech-savvy ways. They need a fearless leader to connect all schools of thought.

Most dealer principles fall into the baby boomer category and value simplicity in personal interactions as well as command and control in their communications. When a Gen Yer fails to return their calls, they take offense, as they grew up returning serve to keep the conversation rolling. They prioritize control, communicating, and responding to needs.

Meanwhile, the typical Internet director tends to be a Gen Y Angry Bird guy flying by the seat of his pants. He takes risks and, if things do not work out, easily separates his job from his life. He ends up being misunderstood and undervalued by the baby boomer Pong players and gets fired.

To bridge the digital divide, I believe the general managers of the next generation will come from Generation X. Despite the misguided perception as a slacker generation and purveyors of the Seattle grunge scene, the leaders of Generation X are best equipped to understand the dynamics of the multitude of generations through the eyes of their employees as well as the eyes of prospective customers. With car shoppers visiting only one to two dealerships before buying, walk-ins no longer happen by chance. Despite the differences in mind-set between baby boomers, Gen X, Y, and Z, the Internet is inherently changing the way in which *everyone* buys cars and does business.

The only way to get people into the door starts with first capturing their interest online. To do that, you need the right person managing your Internet presence. The control-oriented baby boomer leaders may not want to let Gen Y youngsters take control of everything, yet they need to recognize the dynamics at play and the value of a publish-first mind-set. To create a car dog millionaire Internet dealership, you must find talent with a precise skill set: someone who understands every generation's game and plays them with victory in mind. Not the smartest, but the grittiest and most competitive. Someone leadership-oriented with experience both online and on the floor. You need to land this rare breed to turn your store into the best of the bunch. I've come to call these sought after creatures the "fire-breathing dragon tamers."

Fire-breathing dragon tamers are the hardest to find and, when trained, the most lucrative asset a company will have. Since dragon tamers love a challenge, attract them with one. Write a menacing job description that outlines the in-depth responsibilities and ultimate rewards. Instead of getting ten thousand responses, you may only get five. Of those, only one may actually be equipped to tame the dragons while commanding control of your Internet dealership.

Ideally, you want someone with experience as a desk manager, someone who knows how to greet people and run the show. They should be skilled with the Internet, as throwing a rookie into a high-stakes environment can be a fatal flaw. You also want to make sure they have spent some time in finance and insurance and know how to structure deals. Given the expansive prerequisites, you will be browsing through résumés of people on track to be general managers. You need their drive, talent, and experience to excel—compensate them for it.

For these people, running a dealership's Internet sector may sound off the historical track for achieving their goal of becoming a general manager. As the automotive industry continues moving forward, latching onto the Internet and riding along with no intention of going back won't cut it. Rather than turning a career path in the wrong direction, I would argue that experience with the Internet will become—much like F&I is today—a prerequisite for general managers of the future.

To get started in your search for a rock-star Internet sales manager, check out the job description we give to our dealerships. Written five years ago, it has withstood the test of time for attracting the right talent. It outlines all the responsibilities this person will be accountable for in great detail and undoubtedly scares away those ill-fit for the job. You need a go-getter leading your sales team to become a Car Dog Millionaire—stay patient in your search and do not settle.

. . .

INTERNET SALES MANAGER JOB DESCRIPTION

The Internet Sales Manager (ISM) is responsible for receiving and responding to web-based electronic inquiries (leads) and phone calls that result from prospects and customers visiting various Dealership ABC websites. The ISM will be evaluated based on performance standards that measure how many leads were converted to showroom visits and how many of those showroom visits resulted in a sale. The ISM should be fully capable of both traditional and Internet-specific automotive sales processes. The ISM is required to execute customer communications via e-mail, telephone (including VoIP), and face-to-face that conform to the standards and processes put into effect by Dealership ABC management. An ISM must show up for work on time, per published schedules, and conduct himself/herself in a manner compatible with the existing corporate culture and general policies and procedures of Dealership ABC.

Qualifications and Duties include the following:

- Be able to sell cars and trucks using e-mail, phone, and face-to-face skill sets.
- Show up for work on time and as scheduled by manager.
- Attend sales meetings for both the dealership and the Internet department.

- Use a personal computer for e-mail, lead management, website, and MS office applications such as Word, Excel, and Internet Explorer.
- Respond to Internet leads within ten minutes of receiving them.
- Call prospects within thirty minutes of receiving a new lead.
- Set appointments with dealership visits with at least 50 percent of prospects received.
- Achieve lead-to-dealership conversion rate of 14+ percent on new leads received.
- Sell at least 70 percent of prospects who visit the dealership after submitting a new lead.
- Achieve an overall Lead-to-Sales ratio of 10 percent or higher.
- Attend training and complete testing requirements to become certified by ABC's regional office and/or American ABC, USA's national office.
- Use Dealership ABC's lead management systems to ensure response time to all customer inquiries—e-mail, fax, or telephone—is virtually instantaneous.
- Understand the buying patterns and profile of Internet customers.
- Utilize personalized Dealership ABC e-mail templates for communications.
- Utilize Dealership ABC's telephone word tracks as guidelines for process and flow of customer phone contacts.
- Select multiple vehicles for each Internet lead and respond to that lead with price quotes on those vehicles within the first thirty minutes of receiving a new lead.

- Execute Dealership ABC's pricing strategy when responding to leads in a way that profitably competes for the Internet customer both online and offline.

Dealership ABC Websites

- Be thoroughly familiar with the characteristics of all Dealership ABC affiliated websites, as well as those of Dealership ABC lead providers. These sites include:
  - Autotrader.com
  - Cars.com
  - Autobytel
  - Blackbook.com
  - ABC.com
  - Dealix-based websites
  - Outsell leads
  - Blackbook leads
  - Any other sites that may change as business develops
- Know how to use the Lead Management Tool to track customers and to provide updates to the entire organization.
- Learn how to look up inventory data, track vehicle shipments, and locate the desired vehicle for the prospect using ABC technologies.
- Be able to use links to third-party websites in e-mails sent to customers.
- Know how to use Lead Management Tool metrics and reports to improve process performance and sales closing ratios.
- Be comfortable with taking, transferring, and uploading pictures of vehicles as required.

- Execute the Dealership ABC sales process in a consistent yet flexible manner that results in a customer experience designed to achieve the highest quality sales ratios.
- Register all sold customers in ABC programs as required.
- When assigned by general management, directors, or appropriate managers be sure to register, schedule, and attend Internet training and information seminars, including online training, to learn about the latest processes and techniques for interactive business in the automotive industry.
- Attend weekly General Sales Meetings or as otherwise designated.
- Attend weekly Internet Sales Meetings or as otherwise designated.

Measurement and Tracking

- Each day the ISM will complete and electronically submit his or her appointment log and tracking for review by the Business Development and Internet Sales Director.
- Enter all prospect communication notes, records, and customer appointment data into the Dealership ABC Lead Management Tool.
- Track and comply with programs that measure ISM process success including, but not limited to:
  - Leads received.
  - Outbound telephone calls.
  - Appointments set.
  - Appointment shows.
  - Sales.
  - Response time.

- Each ISM must ensure that appointment information is delivered to the enterprise-wide lead tracking system.
- Comply with procedures to ensure that all customers are tracked and follow-up is maintained using the dealership's lead management tools.
- Cooperate with procedures to quality control e-mail and telephone contacts.
- Be open to quantitative as well as qualitative feedback for coaching purposes on recorded phone calls and e-mail communications.
- Maintain tracking boards showing Internet sales updated each day of the month.
- Prepare daily, weekly and monthly reports for review by management as requested.
- Prepare routine reports showing appointments scheduled, which customers showed up, and which customers were sold, as well as where the leads were sourced.

▪ ▪ ▪

Thank you to Ralph Paglia for providing the template for the job description that has been tweaked over time. You too should feel free to tweak this job description to find the right person for your dealership's sales team. For access to each of Local Search Group's other thirty-four dealership job descriptions, visit: www.LocalSearchGroup.com/jobdescriptions.

CHAPTER 5 SUMMARY

Answer: A, Angry Birds

Key Point: When running a dealership, think strategically about how your most influential employees will position you for success. In today's market, the person you hire to run your Internet dealership will directly affect your dealership's sales. Your general manager and Internet director are the two most critical pieces of the puzzle.

Summary:

- Generational games mirror mind-sets and the evolution of people's problem-solving strategies.
- A cauldron of dynamics starts brewing when baby boomers, Gen Xers, Gen Yers, and Gen Zers all mix in the workplace.
  - An ideal leader or general manager understands his or her generation and seeks to understand other generations as well.
  - Anecdotally, Generation X seems to be the best equipped for cross-generational connectivity.
- A dealership's Internet sales manager is becoming one of the most pivotal employees in driving success.
  - To attract a fierce dragon tamer to run your Internet sales department, use a rigorous job description that weeds out people before they apply.

Six

Economies of Fail

6. What term describes a person who fails to live up to his or her early promise?

A Babe in the woods   B. Stick in the mud
C. Flash in the pan   D. Ace in the hole

In May 2008, I met a guy who looked a lot like a dragon tamer. Wicked smart, he worked for a dealership as the Internet sales director and demonstrated serious potential selling online. He strove to be the fastest, strongest player on the team and proved to be an intimidating force. He exercised his talent in a meticulous way—analyzing every aspect of the Internet. He took on not only taming the dragon but also telling stories about it.

He spent time crunching sales ratios and soon became fascinated by the Google algorithm. He Google searched and Google searched every make and model of the cars sold by his dealership to see how they appeared online. He became fixated on the dealership's image, seeing it as an intrinsic part of selling cars. Throughout the week, he would phone my marketing agency and send e-mail after e-mail of urgent online ad ideas and requests.

They went a little something like this:

DRAGON TAMER: *Jim, I made some concerning discoveries here. Googled our "Blizzard Pearl Scion iM" and got NO RESULTS linking back to our dealership. We need a Google AdWords campaign for this ASAP—why do we not already have this?*
JIM: *How many people outside of the employees at your dealership know the color "Blizzard Pearl"?*

. . .

DRAGON TAMER: *Jim, came across our Camry banners online and they looked really unappealing. I threw together this killer one inspired by Late Night with Jimmy Fallon.*
JIM: *How long did that take you?*
DRAGON TAMER: *About five or six hours. Doesn't it look great?*
JIM: *How many car sales happened during that time?*

. . .

DRAGON TAMER: *Hey, I got a lot of likes on the Facebook post I made. It had a picture of a dog driving a car, did you see that one?*

And that's when I knew. I had lost him. Lost him to the dark side of the force otherwise known as the marketing side. When fire breathing dragon tamers start playing on the marketing side, sales go down, they start blaming the environment, and you don't get them back.

This Internet director did do everything he could to manage his dealership's online presence. Attempting to control and endeavoring to influence your external environment in the digital age is a full-time job. Worse yet, when a productive sales associate or leader mistakenly confuses this activity with sales achievement, the ironic unintended consequence is fewer sales. Few dealers have the discipline or understanding of the environment to get the sales director back on task, but when they do, the results are tremendous.

The sales director of this story started spending more of his time crafting the dealership's story than selling cars. As a prime example, he started working on a video to help the dealership go viral. When he tried to conquer marketing, he took his eye off and consequently failed at sales. At the end of the day, selling ratios matter. Critical tasks add to goal achievement, while distractions detract from it.

Though marketing and sales often get clumped together as one, they are two fundamentally different areas of expertise in business. No matter how talented or rock-star-like an employee may be, the flame burns fast in the car business and the all-too-familiar tale of overworked talent and ultimate failure gets told. Recognizing this phenomenon in the car industry, Joe Webb and Bill Playford from DealerKnows Consulting created a comedic YouTube video called "The (De?)Evolution of the Internet Sales Manager."[21]

---

21 *The (De?)Evolution of the Internet Sales Manager* [Motion Picture]. Consulting, D. (Director). Last Modified 2013, https://www.youtube.com/watch?v=eFY2PQiXntQ.

The video starts with a happy Internet sales manager, excited and hopeful about the future. Over the years, he gets thrown more and more responsibility—leads, taking pictures and creating vehicle display pages, website upkeep, daily reports of ROI and closing ratios, sales calls, managing lead providers, SEO and Google AdWords, blogging, and Facebook, YouTube, and Twitter advertising. Eventually, he ends up unhappy and completely overwhelmed in an emotional breakdown.

The moral of that story: adding too many projects to one person's job description slows down momentum rather than moving it forward. To create the most productive work environment for dragon tamers, you must respect their talents and keep them focused. Excelling in sales and marketing requires hiring specialized people in both areas—not one person to do it all. Keep the jobs separate and you will sell more cars, 100 percent guaranteed.

After you hire the dragon tamer to lead Internet sales, start looking for a Walt Disney-type or agency with digital sales operations to lead your marketing team. Ideally, the person you hire for marketing will know how to enchant and tell a good story. In the book *Enchantment: The Art of Changing Hearts, Minds, and Actions*, marketer Guy Kawasaki identifies this trait as a powerful, personal method of persuasion that starts first with a person's likeability and trust.[22] Rather than manipulating customers, the ideal marketer creates a sense of warmth in interactions on the way to becoming a trusted resource. Preconceived notions of distrust already exist in the car industry and overcoming these are typically the first hurdles for all dealership employees. If you

22 Guy Kawasaki, *Enchantment: The Art of Changing Hearts, Minds, and Actions* (Portfolio, 2012).

can start breaking these walls down before people come to the store, then all departments will benefit.

You want someone personable, as the marketing manager will collaborate with people across departments and with your various vendors to build the brand's online image and accomplish the end goal of engaging consumers on the web. They need to operate in a punctual manner and find ways to get back to every internal person every time, with meaningful, timely answers. To learn about other qualifications that make for a great marketer, read through this job description and edit accordingly to recruit talent that fits your needs.

...

MANAGER, INTERACTIVE SALES & MARKETING JOB DESCRIPTION

In this high-profile position, the candidate will assist in the development and execution of strategies to optimize marketing spends and operational sales across all digital platforms, including websites, mobile, and other emerging technologies, with a particular emphasis on leveraging existing technologies that do not require incremental expense. The candidate will interface with corporate and dealership management to communicate performance levels for the platform through routine reporting of Google Analytics, 800 Tracking, Google AdWords, Excel spreadsheets, and other mediums as appropriate.

This position reports to the General Manager of the dealership with heavy daily interaction with the Internet Sales Force of designated dealerships. This position will have responsibility for global interactive content, including web pages, e-mail communications, text campaigns, SEM, SEO, lead generation, classified ads, inventory descriptions, inventory pictures, Internet specials, and other forms of electronic, online, public-facing communication.

The ideal candidate will have the ability to integrate and implement best practices to enrich and enhance the end-user experience, as well as the ability to drive site traffic and manage and expand strategic partnerships to develop online traffic and sales for the dealership. The selected candidate will work with, understand, and actively support the operational dynamics of each market and each dealership in the Family of Dealerships.

The candidate will lead, design, plan, and implement innovative growth opportunities, including potential traffic-building partnerships, mobile, audio, video, and social networking, including and especially the development of Facebook, YouTube, Twitter, LinkedIn, and other social mediums, to authentically engage potential customers. He or she will be involved with management of and oversight of all online editorial content, and will work through Agency Partners to develop an integrated online presence.

QUALIFICATIONS/EXPERIENCE

Relevant digital marketing experience and progressive sales experience is required, including consumer and sales forces interactions as well as business/content traffic tracking. Automotive experience is required. Must have the ability to work in a highly competitive and dynamic environment.

Must be driven and enthusiastic about interactive, mobile media, social media, and emerging digital technologies, with a high level of creativity and the proven ability to develop sales from idea to execution. Excellent cross-departmental people management skills are required. Candidate should have the ability to solve problems through effective communication and interpersonal skills, and the ability to direct and influence resources, as well as the ability to establish and maintain effective working relationships with managers, employees, agencies, manufacturer reps, media, clients, and strategic partners and prospects at all levels.

■ ■ ■

When a qualified person answers your call to join the team as the interactive sales and marketing manager, train him or her to be an elite force. Outline how this person will work with the Internet sales manager, set high expectations, and let the storytelling begin. To get more job descriptions for other roles at your dealership, head over to www.LocalSearchGroup.com/jobdescriptions.

CHAPTER 6 SUMMARY

Answer: C, flash in the pan.

Key Point: An Internet sales manager can't live up to his or her promise if he or she is inundated with too many tasks and projects. To avoid the Internet turning your new hire into a flash in the pan, keep the mission focused on sales. Look for another person—a storyteller—to lead your dealership's marketing.

Summary:

- Adding too many projects to the Internet sales manager's agenda will distract him or her from the ultimate goal of selling cars. Selling ratios matter. That's the job.
- It takes one person to tame a dragon and another to tell the story; you need to hire a strategic person for sales and an enchanting one for marketing.

Seven

Listen Like a Google Whisperer, Profit Like a Car Dog Millionaire

7. What is the art of reading tea leaves called?

A. Tasseography   B. Chado
C. Budoshin   D. Botany

In August of 2012, a Google study found that 90 percent of multidevice consumers switched sequentially between their phones, tablets, and computers to complete tasks.[23] For example, if consumers saw a car they liked on a TV advertisement, they searched to learn more on their smartphone or tablet while sitting on the couch. Later, if still interested, they consulted a computer to continue researching the vehicle.

In a sense, the Internet fundamentally changed the relationship between consumers and products. With reviews readily available and easily accessible, shoppers no longer consumed just products; they first and foremost were consuming information online. With the World Wide Web, mobile devices became the portal.

---

23 "The New Multi-Screen World," Google. Last Modified August 2012, http://services.google.com/fh/files/misc/multiscreenworld_final.pdf.

Soon smartphones started transitioning from a luxury to a necessity. When Apple released their iPhone 5 in 2012, retailers like Best Buy began successful promotions for no money down on the older iPhones.[24] The option to delay responsibility on smartphone payments helped drive what was once a white-collar product into the hands of blue-collar buyers.[25] Today it's clear that iPhones in particular and smartphones in general have replaced the personal computer for most Americans.

As consumers made the shift with ease to using smartphones on the go, personal computers became less and less necessary. By October 2013, Dell announced its move from a publicly traded company to a private one.[26] And one year later, HP split into two different companies, with one for PCs and one for printers.[27] The rush for smartphones drove a simultaneous downturn for desktops.

Recognizing the huge business opportunity in the expanding mobile audience, Google changed its entire advertising platform. The company rolled out "Enhanced Campaigns," a new way for advertisers to better target online consumers across different device types, different geographies, and different day parts.[28] Previously, the search engine optimized ads for desktops, and this

---

24 "Best Buy Black Friday 2012 Deals: Your Shopping Guide," Huffington Post. Last Modified November 22, 2012, http://www.huffingtonpost.com/2012/11/22/best-buy-black-friday-2012-deals_n_2166013.html.

25 "Get That iPhone 5C or 5S Free with Sprint Promotion," McCue, T., Forbes. Last Modified September 16, 2013, http://www.forbes.com/sites/tjmccue/2013/09/16/get-that-iphone-5c-or-5s-free-with-sprint-promotion/.

26 "Dell Officially Goes Private: Inside the Nastiest Tech Buyout Ever," Guglielmo, C., Forbes. Last Modified November 18, 2013, http://www.forbes.com/sites/connieguglielmo/2013/10/30/you-wont-have-michael-dell-to-kick-around-anymore/.

27 "HP to Split into Two Companies," Wallace, G., & Isidore, C., CNNMoney. Last Modified October 6, 2014, http://money.cnn.com/2014/10/06/technology/hp-restructuring-split/.

28 "Enhancing AdWords for a Constantly Connected World," Google. Last Modified February 6, 2013, http://adwords.blogspot.com.br/2013/02/introducing-enhanced-campaigns.html.

was when and where the company made the pivot to focus on mobile. During its studies on consumer behavior, Google observed the frustration that ensued when people tried to access a website that did not load correctly or quickly. When things failed to work efficiently, people lost interest and moved on. Using this research-based insight, Google continued driving businesses to optimize sites for consumers. By January 2015—and with an algorithm that considered time on site, speed of load time, and mobile friendliness—Google owned nearly 75 percent of all US search referrals, according to the StatCounter Global Stats report.[29]

With waves of influence now infiltrating almost every industry, Google directly and indirectly redesigns the way we live. They collect and analyze massive amounts of data; they lead because they listen as they change.

In the search world, Google is the eight-hundred-pound gorilla in the room that businesses cannot ignore. The forward-thinking companies that follow Google closely and take advantage of their tools gain a significant edge on their competition. To take your dealership to the next level, you certainly have to become a Google listener with a mind toward becoming a Google whisperer.

READING THE TEA LEAVES

While reading leaves in tea requires intuitive reflection and some imagination to see what lies ahead, following the future for business starts with watching the experts like Google in systematic ways. When David Barkholz from *Automotive News* listened to my meticulous method for following Google, he confronted me.

---

29 "Yahoo Gains Further US Search Share in January," StatCounter Global Stats. Last Modified February 2015, http://gs.statcounter.com/press/yahoo-gains-further#g1.

"What are you, a Google whisperer or something?" he asked, rather intrigued by it all. "Seems like you, the Kevin Fryes, and Brian Paschs of the world can read the tea leaves that Google is presenting."

I laughed, chalking it up as a compliment. Though the search engine giant sounds daunting, it requires no wizardry, magic, or sixth sense. Powered by data, Google Insights stem from an analytical approach to understanding the digital world. By simply tuning in to their research, you can absolutely learn how to grow your business. The sooner you take advantage of the free tools available, the better off you will be in securing your spot as a Car Dog Millionaire. Start with the following three steps to begin your Google whispering journey.

STEP 1: CHECK YOUR PAGESPEED INSIGHTS

In a world of constant motion, people love clicking, reading, absorbing, sharing, and learning as much information as possible. They love speed and hate waiting. For brands, speed makes the difference between people visiting your page or X-ing it, deciding to buy your product or disregarding it. To help companies build faster websites, the Google team created PageSpeed Insights. By simply entering a URL, Google analyzes the website from a developer's standpoint and gives a score on speed with precise action items for how to fix the things that slow it down.

Share this page with your ISP and marketing manager. From there, devise a team goal to get your speed and user experience to a score of at least an 80 percent. To see the true impact of a faster website, track your current online traffic with an analytic program and watch how it changes with increased efficiency in the consumer experience.

STEP 2: SET UP GOOGLE ANALYTICS

Instruct the dealership's marketing manager to connect Google analytics to the company website. The process is fairly easy and will produce valuable insights on customer behavior as traffic patterns continue to shift from in-person dealership visits to browsing almost exclusively online. Once set up, create weekly check-ins and goals for the marketing manager to track and analyze. Which behaviors on your website are the most highly correlated to the outcomes you want to achieve at the dealership? This will be vital in understanding the Moneyball Factor for your dealership and how web traffic correlates to sales.

If you go through the motions online and avoid tracking behavior, you will miss the Car Dog Millionaire boat. It's the same concept of doing all the work but not printing a financial statement. You couldn't imagine that, nor should you even consider for a second avoiding the necessary tracking components to make the data mean something. Measuring data can be meticulous, yet it gives valuable insight on how and why car shoppers research, compare, and buy. Although a seamless way to join online and offline data is still a dream, there are ways to track both sides. Usually it is not just one channel or medium that influences their car-buying decisions—it results from many channels.

Aside from showing consumer traffic patterns, Google Analytics also features tools that will help you make educated decisions about your marketing spend. Make sure the interactive sales and marketing manager at your dealership digs deeper into these features, including the assisted conversion report.

On your website, you can create goals around what you want visitors to do. Whether you want them to visit the homepage, browse VDPs (vehicle display pages), or fill out a lead form,

Google Analytics lets you enter in these goals. When a visitor completes a specified action, it is called a website conversion. To see how all the marketing channels contribute to your dealership's website conversions, pull up the assisted conversions report. This spreadsheet will break down where all your online traffic is coming from. It uses the terms "assisted conversion" and "last-click/direct conversions" to categorize all the clicks.

Google Definitions

Assisted Conversion: the number and monetary value of sales and conversions the channel assisted. If a channel appears anywhere on a conversion path—except as the final interaction—it is considered an assist for that conversion. The higher these numbers, the more important the assist role of the channel.

Last Click or Direct Conversions: the number and monetary value of sales and conversions the channel closed or completed. The final click or direct traffic before a conversion gets last interaction credit for that conversion. The higher these numbers, the more important the channel's role in driving completion of sales and conversions.[30]

The assisted conversion report illustrates the value of each marketing channel people use to find your business while giving credit to the channels in the early part of the conversion and the last-click/direct conversions. Check out the example assisted conversion report:

---

30 "Analyze channel contribution," Google. Last Modified 2015, https://support.google.com/analytics/answer/1191204?hl=en.

Automotive Sales Channels (?)	Assisted Conversions	Assisted Conversion Value	Last Click or Direct Conversions	Last Click or Direct Conversion Value	Assisted / Last Click or Direct Conversions
1. Direct	3,265 (46.66%)	$28,504.96 (46.39%)	5,594 (46.38%)	$48,934.24 (46.10%)	0.58
2. Organic Search	2,657 (37.97%)	$23,422.24 (38.12%)	4,743 (39.33%)	$42,081.44 (39.64%)	0.56
3. Paid Search	720 (10.29%)	$6,334.40 (10.31%)	1,227 (10.17%)	$10,726.24 (10.10%)	0.59
4. OEM	130 (1.86%)	$1,145.92 (1.86%)	225 (1.87%)	$2,000.80 (1.88%)	0.58
5. Referral	88 (1.26%)	$783.04 (1.27%)	129 (1.07%)	$1,125.92 (1.06%)	0.68
6. Autotrader	40 (0.57%)	$391.04 (0.64%)	48 (0.40%)	$448.80 (0.42%)	0.83
7. (Other)	14 (0.20%)	$120.96 (0.20%)	27 (0.22%)	$233.28 (0.22%)	0.52
8. KBB	46 (0.66%)	$420.16 (0.68%)	26 (0.22%)	$224.64 (0.21%)	1.77
9. Cars.com	19 (0.27%)	$164.16 (0.27%)	21 (0.17%)	$192.80 (0.18%)	0.90
10. Facebook	3 (0.04%)	$25.92 (0.04%)	11 (0.09%)	$95.04 (0.09%)	0.27
11. Edmunds	11 (0.16%)	$95.04 (0.15%)	7 (0.06%)	$60.48 (0.06%)	1.57
12. Group Website	5 (0.07%)	$43.20 (0.07%)	2 (0.02%)	$17.28 (0.02%)	2.50
13. CarFax	0 (0.00%)	$0.00 (0.00%)	1 (0.01%)	$8.64 (0.01%)	0.00

In this example, "Direct Traffic" (when a consumer types your website in the search bar and goes directly to your site or when Google Analytics cannot determine the referrer) gets credit for the majority of traffic. After "Direct Traffic," a large majority of visitors came from "Organic Search" and "Paid Search" listings. Using this directional insight, your next marketing goal would be to tighten up your efforts to drive traffic via these three channels: i.e., you want consumers bookmarking your page, Googling your name, and clicking on your paid search ads because these advertising mediums are driving conversion goals such as seven or more VDP page views, a form fill, or even a phone call.

After looking at the above example, it becomes clear that investments in SEO are important. This dealer is recognizing a $42,081 valuation for his SEO work, even though he spends far less. Paid search is worth $10,726, or about what he's spending on a monthly basis. The OEM website creates $2,000 worth of value. Interestingly, the relative importance of AutoTrader.com and Facebook can be compared. For the $10,000 plus the dealer spent on AutoTrader, the return on his website is $448… not much more than Facebook, where the dealer spent closer to $500 dollars.

As a dealer, if you spend significantly more money on third-party lead providers only to get ostensibly the same results, it's worth reconsidering how you allocate your resources. Importantly, you must also understand the value that their website is giving you. With tracking resources like vAuto, you can value the VDPs you receive from AutoTrader.com or Cars.com. VDPs are worth what you pay for them, so understanding the relative costs for each is important.

Putting a Value on the Conversion

To connect the traffic data and determine the ROI for your marketing efforts, you need to put a value on the conversion. You can either assign the same value to all conversion actions (static values), or let a conversion action have different values (transaction specific).

How do you find your value per conversion?

1. Figure out how much money you are spending on advertising.
2. Determine how much money you are making in gross profit in that department.

If the dealership spent $100,000 on advertising and delivered 100,000 VDPs, I'll set the value of VDP to $1 because that's what it costs. What are your numbers?

If you don't know your numbers but want to get started, the industry standard value is $8 for a VDP.

Goal Setting

In your analytics, you will also want to set measurable goals. Use the following goals as a guide:

Form Visit
Form Visit—Blackbook
Form Visit—Credit Score Estimator
Form Visit—Get a Quote
Form Visit—Instant Credit Score

Homepage Visit
Vehicle Detail Page View
Viewed Hours and Directions
Viewed Service Appointment Page

STEP 3: CREATE GOOGLE ALERTS

Becoming a Google whisperer means not only using Google's resources but also listening closely to how they choose to index the things you share. To monitor your presence online, create a Google Alert for your dealership name. By doing so, you and/or your marketing manager will receive e-mails when your dealership name appears anywhere on the web. This gives you awareness of your current reputation and how people are perceiving and talking about you and your brand.

At one point in my Google Alerts tracking, I noticed that my dealerships were starting to index on reviews from various sites on the web. Google began picking up consumer feedback on sites like DealerRater, Yelp, Merchant Circle, LinkedIn, Yahoo, and Bing, in addition to their own site. Shortly thereafter, the various review websites started showing up on the first page for not only our dealer group but the entire dealer nation. Now utilizing the wisdom of the masses, I knew it was time to clean up all our dealer reviews (for more on reputation management, flip to Chapter 15).

In addition to tracking your dealership, adding your competitors' names to your Google Alerts can help you stay up to speed with what they are doing in the increasingly digital world and community that we live in. Start first by setting up a few alerts for local competitors, and use their successes and mistakes to steer your own dealership in the right direction.

As industry leaders like Jim Ziegler, Shaun Raines, and Dennis Galbraith can attest, the art of becoming a Google whisperer requires you to take advantage of current market resources while simultaneously looking forward to the future. To truly capture the essence of a whisperer, you must closely follow the leaders, look for cues, and pay attention to their plans.

While Google leads the world in search, Facebook leads the world in social. Though both are extremely powerful entities for different reasons, they are not collaborating together. Instead, there is an interesting dynamic shaping each entity: Google is trying to become more socially adept, and Facebook is trying to become more search oriented.

The evolution of these organizations will continue to have a direct influence on how you advertise and interact with consumers. Right now, Google is taking nearly 75 percent of the search market, but the other sites like Bing and Yahoo are edging forward and looking to grab more of their fair share. If you forget about them, your competitors will not. Keep these other search engines on your radar, and think of them as clunkier, less sexy cars. You might not want to cruise around in them, but every now and again get behind the wheel to make sure they are running properly in your efforts to go from point A (Car Dog) to point B (Car Dog Millionaire). If you and your team tune in, you will be the first to know about new tools and resources that will continue to—as they have ironically done so in the past—effectively predict the future of our business.

GOOGLE ANAYLTICS CASE STUDY

Google Analytics also provides other compelling information and can help you determine how to mash up your marketing mix. Take a look at this unique insight from a different dealer in the "Traffic Sources" section of Google Analytics.

Source/Medium	Aquistion			Behavior	
	Sessions	% New Sessions	% New Users	Bounce Rate	Pages/Session
	10,493	**70.29%**	**7,376**	**45.96%**	**4.43**
	% of Total: 100% (10,493)	Avg. for View: 70.22% (0.11%)	% of Total: 100.11% (7,368)	Avg for View: 45.96% (0.00%)	Avg for View: 4.43 (0.00%)
1. etechtrack / email	**2,624** (25.01%)	98.97%	2,597 (35.21%)	52.55%	2.22
2. google / organic	**4,448** (23.33%)	52.41%	1,283 (17.39%)	23.53%	7.03
3. (direct) / (none)	**2,413** (23.00%)	71.11%	1,716 (23.26%)	62.58%	4.08
4. google / cpc	**1,827** (17.41%)	62.67%	1,145 (15.52%)	55.06%	4.13
5. LSG + Bing / cpc	**203** (1.93%)	78.33%	159 (2.16%)	34.98%	4.11

Notice how e-mail drove the most traffic during this period and delivered 98.97 percent worth of new sessions. As a marketer, this insight is incredibly valuable. Many dealers use e-mail through their CRM only, and it is a great way to stay connected with current customers. However, dealers that want to move the needle are realizing there's a whole new world of prospects available when e-mail marketing is done the right way.

CHAPTER 7 SUMMARY

Answer: A, Tasseography

Key Point: The art of reading tea leaves involves some intuitive reflection to understand where you are at and what the future holds. Though Google whispering sounds like an art of fortune-telling, it's more or less about keeping your head on a swivel with a data-based approach to moving your company forward.

Summary:

- The Internet is changing the relationship between consumers and products with people now consuming information first and foremost. We are no longer in the Industrial Age.
- The rise in smartphones as a necessity led to a corresponding downturn in desktops.
- Speed is a vital factor in converting web surfers to customers.
- Become a Google whisperer with three key steps:
  - Check Google's PageSpeed Insights
  - Set up Google Analytics and multichannel funnels
  - Create and track Google Alerts
- While Google still captures about three-quarters of the search market, a quarter of the online users are browsing on other search engines like Yahoo and Bing. Pay attention to the opportunities available as they begin the process of separating and then ultimately growing.

Eight

From Kicking Tires to Clicking Tires with Digital Dealerships

8. If two variables are highly correlated, what do you know?

A. They always go together.

B. High values on one variable lead to high values on the other variable.

C. There are no other variables the relationship.

D. Changes in one variable are accompanied by predictable responsible for by changes in the other.

A man lounges in his recliner in the zone as he watches the cars of a Formula One race zoom by. During a commercial break, an advertisement for the new Ram truck catches his eye. He pulls out his phone and does a quick Google search on the truck. He clicks to a local dealership and finds a page with a few pictures but no price—just a line to "call for more information."

Vrooooom vroom. His vague interest fades as coverage for Formula One speeds back on. Much later, long after the races end, he remembers the truck and searches again on his tablet. The first link he clicks on for the vehicle leads him to the home page of a local dealer's website—not to the Ram—so he goes back and tries another link.

The next one doesn't load right on his tablet. He clicks back and hopes the third time will be the charm. This site looks better. He browses around on it for a few minutes. To do more serious research, he decides to jump on his laptop. He pulls up the last website that he felt satisfied with alongside a new window that he opens for AutoTrader.com. The pictures on AutoTrader show the truck sitting in a muddy lot, making it look more like a used car than a new one. The other website has professional photos of the truck that look crisp, clean, and brand-new. He clicks around to browse through the library of images, details, and pricing.

In total, he visits seven-plus pages for this truck on the dealer's website. And luckily for this dealer, seven is the magic number. According to our research with retail car dealers, when a visitor shops inventory online and clicks through more than seven VDPs on average, his or her behavior changes from browsing to buying and the shopper becomes statistically correlated to a vehicle sale.

With car shoppers going from kicking tires in lots to clicking tires online, VDPs are the most highly correlated variable to consumer buying behavior. To better understand how the statistics correlate, we will be diving into some sample dealership data. Though it seems intuitive that more people shopping your website inventory would translate to more car sales, the numbers paint an even more powerful picture. To lay the groundwork for our research, let's first begin with the basics and define correlations.

A **positive correlation** exists when two variables move in tandem; when one variable decreases, the other variable also decreases, and vice versa. A perfect positive correlation is represented numerically in statistics with +1.

Example: The more gasoline you put in your car, the farther it can go.

A **negative correlation** exists among two variables when one variable increases as the other decreases, and vice versa. In statistics, -1 represents a perfect negative correlation.

Example: The more time I spend at my dealership, the less time I spend with my family.

To understand online car shopping behavior, we looked at the Google Analytics data for one of our dealerships over a three-month period. On average, roughly 30,000 people visited their website each month. At first glance, 1,000 visitors a day seemed like an incredible amount of traffic. We knew some people were visiting only one page and bouncing, while others were clicking around and taking their time.

To break it down further, we split up the website traffic by session behavior. Each session represents a visit from a user with a unique IP address during a specific period of time. We wanted to see what kind of behavior occurred when people looked at VDPs and how they behaved in sessions where they did not look at VDPs.

AVERAGE MONTHLY SESSIONS ON DEALERSHIP WEBSITE

Website Sessions	
With VDP Views	12,376
Without VDP Views	20,197
Total	32,573

For each session with and without VDP views, how many pages were visitors looking at? We broke down the data even further:

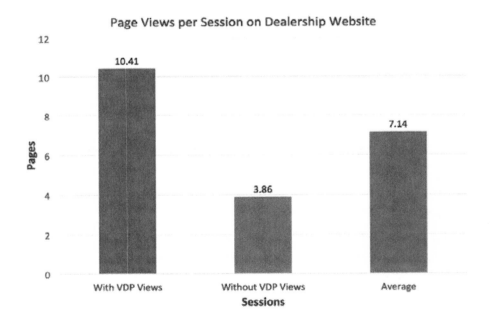

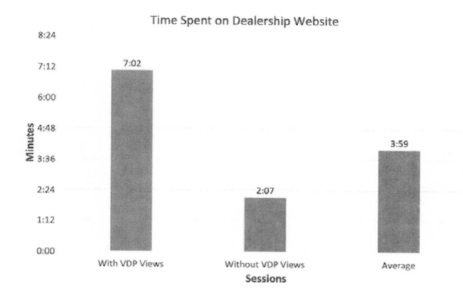

On average, a website visitor looking at VDPs clicked through about ten pages and spent roughly seven minutes on the dealership website. A visitor who did not look at VDPs spent only two minutes on the site.

Once a consumer clicked through more than 7.14 pages, he or she was over the average threshold for browsing and entered into the buying behavior category. The more pages the consumer was looking at, the more likely it was that he or she was going to buy a car. After discovering the correlation of VDPs and sales for this one dealership, we continued our research and ran the same calculations for eleven more dealerships. From there we found the magic number: across the board, roughly 7.23 VDP page views correlated positively to car sales.

We then looked at a different set of five dealerships to see if our theory held true. At a + 0.96 correlation, the data continued to reveal that VDPs were positively correlated to car sales.

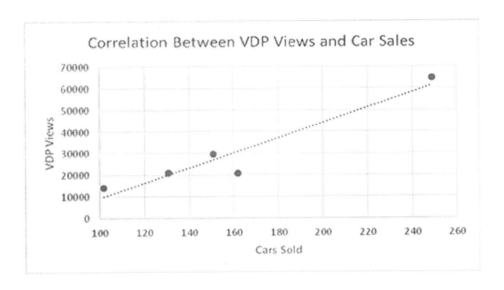

Driving people to the website is a fundamental consideration, yet Car Dog Millionaires set conversions around the behaviors that drive sales. People who hit a site and leave do not show the same intent to buy cars as the ones staying around to browse. Dealers who thought of the secondary consideration—getting people to use their webpages as resources for information—are the ones who are grabbing market share and customers.

Using a Car Dog Millionaire mind-set with finite yet powerful budgets, I went to the next level to help determine what valuation I was receiving from my vendor partners. With car dealers paying to share their inventory in a few different places, including AutoTrader and Cars.com, we wanted to determine which VDP traffic proved to be the most valuable. My team then looked at the same twelve dealerships and analyzed the VDP page views from their website, AutoTrader, and Cars.com.

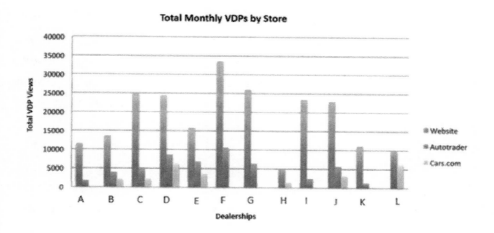

Out of the twelve dealerships, ten had website VDP views that far surpassed traffic from AutoTrader and Cars.com. Keeping this finding in mind, we took a closer look at the cost per VDP for each of these sites based on the self-reported investments being made.

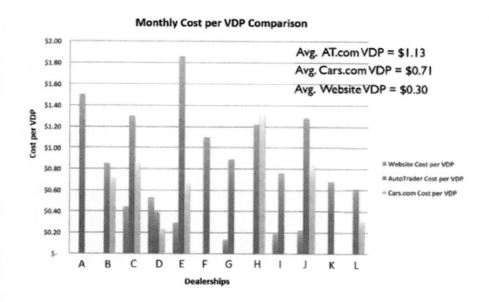

For every dealership we studied, the cost for VDPs on AutoTrader greatly exceeded the costs for Cars.com and dealer websites, which cost the least. Ten years ago, AutoTrader had an advantage in technology capabilities, so dealers paid a premium to be part of the community. Yet over the past five years, technology has leveled. Now more affordable technology allows local dealerships to build their own websites with functionality similar to AutoTrader, without paying the additional costs. In my studies, money spent on AutoTrader is no longer positively correlated to car sales in the ever-changing digital world.

In fact, from a statistical viewpoint, costs on AutoTrader are now becoming negatively correlated to car sales in some instances: meaning, the *more* money you spend on AutoTrader, the *less* volume you sell. AutoTrader is a great company, but this is one of the changing patterns in the digital plate tectonics that make up our Internet dealerships. When consumers search on AutoTrader, the site automatically sorts the results from high to low prices. From there, users re-sort from low to high in order to find the cheapest vehicles. As a car dealer, this means you are paying a premium to have your cars listed on a website where customers are asking for the cheapest deal. When you compete against other dealers and lower your prices, you make less profit per every unit you sell.

JIM: *As Car Dog Millionaires have likely heard, volume is for vanity and profit is for sanity!*

Carefully invest your dollars and understand how AutoTrader works for your market. From a return on investment standpoint, throwing money at AutoTrader may or may not translate into more profit or car sales. The good news, on the other hand, is that SEO is theoretically free, and any traffic you drive to your website creates a stronger return on investment. Instead of competing next to other dealers, you compete only against yourself and make more gross profit per unit on your website.

In all my 20 Group presentations through the years, I've yet to hear a dealer tell me that they are more profitable on third-party lead providers than they are on their own website (or first-party lead). Now some have said that they don't know, but conventional wisdom says that first-party leads are more profitable.

As you look at the following chart, know that I ran the correlations and regressions for each of the makes, models, and markets that are reported, and what I've found is that "Avg. VDPs of Visitors to Website" is the most predictive of vehicle sales...more so than "Total VDPs" even, which isn't correlated. Say what? Can't be right. Volume predicts volume, right? Except when it doesn't, which makes this chapter even more important.

The things you do to drive more vehicle display page views per visitor will drive vehicle volume. It's the new reality in the car business that many old-school Car Dogs still don't want to accept. In the car business for decades, activity resulted in achievement. The bolder the better! Big gorillas on rooftops! Massive American flags! Huge four-page color newspaper spreads! Sunday! Sunday! Sunday! Everywhere on the TV! Relentlessly repetitive, screamer spots on the radio! Except now in the digital realm, where time is the most precious commodity consumers have, anyone can get the information about the car they want when they want it.

Now dealers should allocate time, effort, and energy to be the location where someone goes to when he or she wants to take a look at vehicles. Early adopters of this philosophy have invariably come out ahead. In their book *Zero to Sixty Million: Under the Hood of the World's Largest eBay Motors Dealer*, Mike Welch and Rick Williams describe how they went from selling zero cars a month to over four hundred cars a month in only four years, with no previous car experience. If you bother to take a look at their site, you will notice that the pictures of the cars are impeccable. Bright lights and fantastic photos helped set the early stage and standard for vehicle viewability. It translated into vehicle sales for them ahead of the curve and during the downturn mentioned in Chapter 1.

Correlation to Total Vehicle Sales

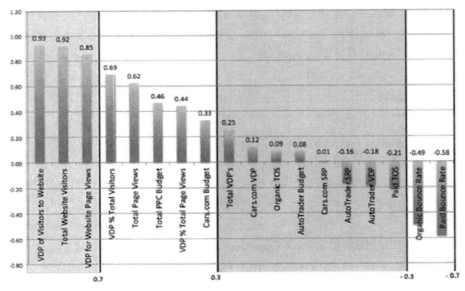

Today, in order to maximize earning potential for your Internet dealership, you must drive the average number of VDPs per user up. Most would agree that more traffic with high bounce rates isn't value adding. It's what we move away from in our advertising efforts. But flipped upside down, what should you be moving toward? In your advertising and marketing mediums, if you are discussing and allocating resources to drive average VDPs per visitor up, you will have a better investment, you will lower your cost per sale, and you will be on your way to Car Dog Millionaire status.

Additionally, if you are on AutoTrader and Cars.com, you should be aware of the VDP count for each site. These numbers will reveal how strong each platform is relative to your retail efforts and getting your cars in front of consumers. Compare these numbers to the VDP views from your dealership website.

Also keep in mind that you can disregard the search results page (SRP) count on AutoTrader and Cars.com. Statistically and intuitively, it doesn't matter how high this number is. At the end of the day, VDPs matter more than SRPs in your effort to sell more cars.

DATA TOOL TIP

Use software tools like vAuto to compare and contrast your dealership against AutoTrader and Cars.com. Work hard to compare apples to apples and oranges to oranges. There are some huge differences that are important understand; in particular how new car VDPs and used car VDPs behave on those two sites as well as your own should be considered. Those measures will be unique to your makes, your models, and your markets. Taking the time to drive your thinking and the thinking for your team around this will help you shape your selling strategies.

DOS AND DON'TS OF VDPS

To create compelling website VDPs, give your consumers exactly what they are looking for: pictures, prices, and descriptions. Use the following as guidelines for building your inventory webpages.

Pictures

Do:

- Make sure images are lossless and compressed; details are important, but so are load times.
- Use Evox images for new cars, as people want perfection.
- Take twenty or more photos for used cars, or as many as your vendor will provide at no cost.
- Invest in a place where natural light can be controlled, as shadows hurt gross.
- Capture all used car images on well-lit, clear days if a controlled lighting environment isn't available.
- Put your dealer URL in the background of the image. Some inventory scrapers will grab your photos to sell leads back to you. Without your URL or some identifying aspect, you'll be at the mercy of the lead provider.

Don't:

- Take pictures of new cars on your lot.
- Create noise in pictures of your used cars with distractions in the background like mud, snow, weather, AC leaks, or lack of sunlight.
- Spend too much time and money on superfluous photos.

Prices

Do:

- Price competitively and show it transparently.
- Update and adjust prices weekly with vAuto.
- Seek to understand your inventory and your competitors.

Don't:

- Put "Call for price." People will eliminate you from the consideration set.
- Leave money on the table by not adjusting prices with the market.

Descriptions

Do:

- Display content with all relevant car facts and features.
- Use the vAuto for custom descriptions.

Don't:

- Write cheesy and aggressive: BUY NOW! TODAY! HURRY!
- Overinvest in SEO for noncore used car inventory. If you buy this, you've been sold. Used cars are only around for sixty days anyway. Fast turns don't allow for SEO on used cars—at least not in Google's world.

VDP GOAL SETTING

Once all your VDPs are revamped, the Internet sales director and marketing manager should set strategic goals. With the industry rule of thumb to never hold a used car longer than sixty days in mind, focus on website VDPs as a means to get cars off the lot. Set goals around the following:

1. More used VDPs equals more car sales.

Goal: For every 250 VDP page views, sell one used car.

2. For new cars, less is more.

Goal: For every 100 VDP page views, sell one new car.

Track, measure, and adjust for the performance with your makes, your models, and your markets. The key is establishing the benchmark for your future success.

CHAPTER 8 SUMMARY

Answer: D, if two variables are highly correlated, we know that changes in one variable are accompanied by predictable changes in the other.

Key Point: Through our research, we found that VDPs are highly correlated with car sales, such that when VDP page views per visitor increase, car sales predictably increase as well.

Summary:

- In my research, 7.23 VDPs per visitor represents the threshold at which potential shoppers become buyers.
- Money spent on AutoTrader is often not correlated with car sales. Check your market.
- VDP views are positively correlated with car sales.
  - Well-crafted VDPs feature pristine pictures, transparent prices, and comprehensive descriptions.
  - Set ambitious VDP goals, then track, then shift goals, and then continue to measure.
    - For every 250 VDP page views, sell one used car.
    - For every 100 VDP page views, sell one new car.

Nine

Car Shoppers Love Their Cell Phones—You Should, Too

9. Who said, "Give me a lever long enough and a fulcrum on which to place it, and I shall move the world?"

A. Alexi

B. Archimedes

C. Plato

D. Cardone

By the end of 2015, there will be more than seven billion mobile cell phone subscriptions worldwide, according to the United Nations (UN) Agency on Telecommunications.[31] With the global population at 7.3 billion, cell phones are penetrating nearly 97 percent of the world.[32] Mind-blowingly, there are almost as many cell phone subscriptions as there are people on Earth.

The UN agency also projects mobile-broadband subscriptions to penetrate 47 percent of the globe by the end of 2015.

31 "The World in 2015: ICT Facts and Figures," International Telecommunication Union. Last Modified May 2015, http://www.itu.int/en/ITU-D/Statistics/Documents/facts/ICTFactsFigures2015.pdf.

32 "World Population Projected to Reach 9.7 Billion by 2050," United Nations Department of Economic and Social Affairs. Last Modified July 29, 2015, http://www.un.org/en/development/desa/news/population/2015-report.html.

With participation levels twelve times higher than in 2007, mobile Internet is becoming the most dynamic information, communication, and technology platform in the world, and advertisers are following.

Since Marty Cooper prototyped the first mobile phone in 1973 and brought it to the US market with Motorola in 1983, cell phones have integrated rapidly into consumers' lives.[33] Today, the one-on-one medium continues to create a unique connection between people and brands, giving users open access to information and advertisers direct access to their audiences.

To capitalize on the increasingly mobile world, Google designed AdWords Enhanced Campaigns—a platform to optimize the relationship for both consumers and brands. It allows businesses to hypertarget mobile ads and, in turn, strengthens user experiences with precisely relevant ads within the corresponding geography and/or time of day.

Since Google knows that all clicks are not created equal, Enhanced Campaigns also gives advertisers bidding options to amplify their voice and gain control over when and where their ads will be shown. Bid amplification with these campaigns works similarly to the way speakers amplify sound. For instance, when you are sitting in a quiet house, you can hear your favorite song as it plays softly on your phone. When you throw a house party, people crowd the space with noise and opinions—forcing you to compete for the next song in the playlist queue. When you finally get your air time, you must crank the external speakers up to amplify the volume. Sometimes you have to pay DJs to get the song you want when you want it.

---

33 "Father of the Cell Phone," *The Economist*. Last Modified June 4, 2009, http://www.economist.com/node/13725793?story_id=13725793.

As for bids, when you advertise in a quiet space, your bid will stay at a minimum like the volume of your favorite song being played on your phone. When the space becomes crowded with companies that want impression share, people will compete for and pay more to be heard, thus increasing the stakes.

If you want your voice to be heard over your competitors, Google lets you amplify your bid up to 300 percent for mobile traffic. The search giant realizes the value in mobile users clicking and searching for fast information, and wants to let people compete for it. If a competitor wants the same traffic and has the same quality score and same maximum cost per click but is only willing to amplify its bid by 200 percent, your ad will show. Economic theory states that value increases with demand, so the price you pay for each click could be up to three times higher than your max cost per click (CPC) depending on your competitive environment. Thank goodness dealers aren't competitive!

For example, say you set a max CPC of $1 for people Google searching "Honda Car Dealership" on their mobile phones. Then you set your amplification percentage at 300 percent. If other companies are competing for the same words at this level, the max CPC you could pay would be: $1 CPC x 300 percent = $3.

Google also lets you multiple your bids for geography and time of day by 900 percent to help you cater to your direct market during the most interactive hours. Overall, the bid percentages create a market where the advertisers willing to pay the most secure the available spots to be shown. For businesses, the real fun begins when their marketing teams figure out how to use tech-savvy Google knowledge to out-execute the competition and play the loudest song at the party.

OUTSMARTING THE OTHER GUY

In February (which is otherwise a short-selling month), many dealers begin the process of ramping up for spring selling season. One of my dealer clients called me up feeling pretty peeved about another guy encroaching on his territory and stealing customers from his dealership. He wanted to figure out how to take down the competition. The prior year he had finished number one in his market, but to start the new calendar year, this annoying, persistent competitor had started showing up more frequently in searches for his name and had started moving up the sales-ranking reports. His competitor's retail game and advertising were strong, but ours was stronger. As a Google whisperer, I had a few ideas for how to put my dealer in the lead again.

DEALER: *I want to get in his head.*
JIM: *In his head. Understood.*
DEALER: *No, I mean IN HIS head.*
JIM: *Got it. In his head!*
DEALER: *Like, I want this guy to wonder what he ever did to me to make me so focused on him.*
JIM: *Like you want him to give up?*
DEALER: *Kinda. No, not have him give up. Really I want him to know that I WILL NOT give up. That he's in my crosshairs. That I operate like a military spy and that he will not able to rest. I want him to consider whether or not he should go to sleep at night because when he wakes up he will be wondering what I'm doing.*
JIM: *So you want to be number one for his name in Google searches?*
DEALER: *That's good. How much?*

JIM: *Well, I have something new.*
DEALER: *Tell me how much.*
JIM: *Google launched this thing called Enhanced Campaigns. It goes into full effect in July, but for now it's completely optional. Most companies are waiting until July to implement, but we're ready.*
DEALER: *What is this thing you call Enhanced Campaigns?*
JIM: *You can amplify your max Google bids according to geography and time of day, and by mobile device—900 percent up for the first two, 300 percent up for mobile.*
DEALER: *Will this make me number one for his name?*
JIM: *Depends on what you are willing to spend.*
DEALER: *I don't want to break the bank. I want to outmaneuver him.*
JIM: *Let's try this. Let's target a two-mile radius around his dealership and buy only his name.*
DEALER: *What will it cost?*
JIM: *Not much until he figures out what you are doing; then it depends on how he responds.*
DEALER: *OK, put a thousand behind it and keep an eye on it.*
JIM: *On it.*

Two months later.

JIM: *Looks like we woke the sleeping giant.*
DEALER: *What do you mean?*
JIM: *Remember that dealer we targeted with your name? Well, he had been showing up number two quite frequently—if not all the time—for his name because*

we were willing to amplify your max bid by 900 percent around his dealership.

DEALER: *Remind me.*

JIM: *Remember the deal where you wanted your competitor to know that you operated with surgical precision...like a military operation? He figured out that you were buying his name.*

DEALER: *Oh, yeah [smiling]. What did he do?*

JIM: *Well, we got in his head.*

DEALER: *Great.*

JIM: *He started buying your name, and then he started to bid on his own name to see how high he would have to go before he would become number one. See, I have this chart from Google that shows that he did all this work on April 20. So he clicked on bids for your name. One bid at a time.*

DEALER: *So he spent a day figuring this out?*

JIM: *At least. Probably weeks. He finally decided to spend the money to figure it out. Also, you were outrunning him for two months on this.*

DEALER: *How much did it cost me?*

JIM: *We never went over budget, but it did cost $50 for one click.*

DEALER: *WHAT?*

JIM: *Your max CPC was $5 and with 900 percent amplification around his dealership geography along with 300 percent amplification for mobile, we were always willing to pay that to stay number one. We just didn't have to pay that until he decided he was willing to pay that to be number one as well.*

DEALER: *This is amazing. So what's going on now?*
JIM: *I've looked at searches across the city now. He got back into the game and is going after you all over the town. From what I can tell, though, he can't compete on a citywide basis. Too expensive. You are only competing around his store.*
DEALER: *This is so awesome. What can we do next?*

THE NOW GOOGLE FEATURE: CALL-ONLY CAMPAIGNS

In February 2015, two years after rolling out Enhanced Campaigns, Google announced their new Call-Only Campaigns.[34] This feature allows advertisers to reach customers with ads specifically designed to encourage people to call—a vital step for businesses like car dealerships that value leads over website clicks. As the next competitive edge, Call-Only Campaigns ensure visibility to consumers and easy access to the most important business information, including the description, phone number, and a call button.

For dealers, the final transaction must happen at their lot, and they need to make it as easy as possible for car shoppers to get there. Call-Only Campaigns create a unique solution, as they are hypertargeted to show up only on mobile devices that can make phone calls. Imagine a shopper researching cars, switching from her phone to laptop and finally figuring out what car she wants to buy. The next day, she decides to head to a dealership to check it out in person. She jumps in her car in the garage and does a quick Google search on her phone to verify the address of the closest dealer.

---

34 "Charge Up Your Phones with Call-Only Campaigns," Google. Last Modified February 20, 2015, http://adwords.blogspot.com.br/2015/02/charge-up-your-phones-with-call-only.html

For dealerships, visibility in this micromoment makes the difference between a car sale and a marketing fail. If a dealership is not listed as one of the first options for car shoppers on the go, they lose their place in the competition. If listed, dealers up their chances significantly for selling the car. Remember, with car shoppers only visiting 1.6 dealerships before buying, they either buy at the first place or close the deal at the second.

The specialized bidding options of Call-Only Campaigns allow advertisers to design campaign strategies based around call goals. With each ad focused on a single call to action of making a phone call, every click you pay for can be a call to your dealership. Thanks to Google, you can now ensure your dealership's visibility in the most crucial part of the consumer buying path—when the customer is ready to buy.

CHAPTER 9 SUMMARY

Answer: B, Archimedes

Key Point: Today, mobile Internet is the most dynamic information and communication technology; it is the lever to move the world. Using Google's Enhanced Campaigns and Call-Only features will allow your dealership to connect with consumers through mobile Internet.

Summary:

- By the end of 2015, cellular subscriptions will penetrate 97 percent of the world. It's where the people are, and advertisers are following.
- To help advertisers reach consumers through mobile devices, Google created Enhanced Campaigns, which lets businesses create ads and amplify bids to compete for prime traffic.
  - Advertisers can multiply their bid by 300 percent for mobile and 900 percent for geography and time of day.
- Google's Call-Only Campaigns let you create ads that show up only for mobile phone users, feature a call button, and make your dealership accessible to shoppers on the go.
- Tuning in to Google's innovation will help you outsmart your competition online and finish ahead of the pack with car sales at your dealership.

Ten

Set Smart Goals to Avoid Getting Lost at Sea

10. What Atlantic region did five US Navy Avenger airplanes mysteriously vanish from while passing through?

A. Paglia's Place

B. Suzuki's Sea

C. Hurricane Bay

D. Bermuda Triangle

O n December 5, 1945, US Navy Flight 19 was scheduled for a routine three-hour training mission from Fort Lauderdale, Florida. The squadron of torpedo bombers would travel due east 120 miles, north for 73 miles, and then 120 miles back to the naval base.[35] However, two hours after the five Avenger planes took off, the leader of the squadron reported his compass and backup compass were malfunctioning. The radio facilities on land were also unable to locate them. After hours of confused messages, the squadron leader was heard over a muffled radio ordering his men to abort their aircraft due to a fuel shortage.

---

35 "1945 Aircraft Squadron Lost in the Bermuda Triangle," History.com. Last Modified (n.d.). Retrieved September 8, 2015, http://www.history.com/this-day-in-history/aircraft-squadron-lost-in-the-bermuda-triangle.

Speculating the squadron to be somewhere east of Florida and north of the Bahamas, a search-and-rescue Mariner aircraft took off to find them. The rescue crew radioed to the home base three minutes into the mission, and the Mariner plane was never heard from again.

Despite a massive air and sea search that involved hundreds of ships and aircraft covering thousands of miles from the Gulf of Mexico to the Atlantic, no bodies or planes were ever found. Twenty-seven men and their aircraft vanished mysteriously in the area now known as the Bermuda Triangle.

The legends of this mythical section of the Atlantic Ocean date all the way back to Christopher Columbus, who wrote about erratic compass readings there on his first voyage to the New World—perhaps due to north and magnetic north lining up in that area at the time. Since then, a wide range of theories from sea monsters to gas eruptions in the ocean floor have emerged, yet none of the proposed theories solve the mystery of ship or plane disappearances over the area. Even the US Coast Guard said, "In a review of many aircraft and vessel losses in the area over the years, there has been nothing discovered that would indicate that casualties were the result of anything other than physical causes. No extraordinary factors have ever been identified."[36] If the pilots and captains were well aware of the geography and weather conditions of this stretch of the Atlantic, they should have been able to pass through just fine.

---

36 "Coast Guard History Frequently Asked Questions," US Coast Guard. Last Modified November 17, 2014, http://www.uscg.mil/history/faqs/triangle.asp.

SPEAKING OF UNEXPLAINED MYSTERIES...

Advertising budgets can be a misunderstood part of a dealership's operations. Through the years, people relied on gut decisions and received healthy rewards for "spray and pray behavior"—spending their dollars all over the place and hoping it somehow brought in more business. As more and more advertising mediums emerged at the same time that finances tightened, dealers and general managers began the process of balancing budgets with the need to get to the right place at the right time. Instead of saving their way to glory, smart dealers and their marketing agencies worked on calculated plans to allocate dollars and track returns. If a dealership spent money without knowing what to look for afterward, a lot of dollars could be thrown into the ocean, never to be seen again.

Today, defining an advertising budget for your dealership starts first with acknowledging the environment. Before you can even think about spending a dime on marketing, it is imperative to understand the following assumptions about the automotive landscape:

1. **Shopping doesn't happen at the store.** For most retail businesses, consumer browsing and shopping happens online. Yet for the automotive industry, *buying* still happens at the dealership. As we move forward, car dealers are required to be problem solvers in both online and offline spaces. Consider stores like Macy's and Nordstrom as excellent examples of this; they excel with both a really good retail location and a really great online buying environment.

2. **Sales tracking starts at your website.** Dealers used to think sales tracking started with their CRM by looking at

the number of phone calls and people who showed up at their dealerships. Now car shoppers are showing up first on dealer websites, albeit electronically. As a result, website analytics have become a more accurate indicator to track sales (flip back to Chapter 3 for more on that).

3. **Online car transactions will happen someday. Soon.** Though most state laws and motor vehicle commissions don't allow for cars to be purchased online today, I believe it will happen soon enough. The technology certainly exists. Look at what's possible with Amazon and know that technology companies like Apple and Google are already working on electric vehicles and driverless cars.[37]

THE AUTOMOTIVE BERMUDA TRIANGLE

As a dealership, your initial goal is to drive people to your website. If you believe this to be true and agree with the above three assumptions, then we are on the same page and it's time to talk about the "Automotive Bermuda Triangle."

To avoid wasting your money and missing your sales goals, take the time to learn the theory of the Automotive Bermuda Triangle: the relationship between your personnel, inventory, and website visitors. Understanding this relationship can guide you to sales success with less than five minutes of effort each month. These checkpoints help ensure that you have the right number of cars and people to handle the amount of traffic you want to bring to your dealership. They will also be the guiding force for setting your advertising budgets.

INVENTORY
Know the cars on your lot and in your pipeline. This is a vital, rudimentary step for dealerships. Also recognize the velocity at which you sell vehicles over the course of two months. For a good ballpark estimate on how many cars you should sell as a goal, take the number of cars on the ground at the beginning of the month and divide it by two. If your turn rate is faster, move the number accordingly.

Inventory Formula
of cars on ground ÷ 2 = # of cars to sell (goal)

Example: If you have 300 cars on your lot this month, your goal should be to sell 150 of them.
300 cars ÷ 2 = 150 cars

Dealers who try to sell every vehicle in their inventory each month are pushing for unrealistic goals. Adding more money into advertising will not lead to more sales if you do not have team members available to accept new business and sell those cars.

PERSONNEL

Personnel includes the revenue-generating individuals who routinely show up to work—or as I like to call them, your motivated salespeople. On average, car salespeople sell ten vehicles a month.[38]

Personnel Formula

of cars to sell ÷ 10 cars/person = # of salespeople needed

Example: If you want to sell 200 vehicles this month, you need to have at least 20 salespeople.
200 cars ÷ 10 cars/person = 20 salespeople

WEBSITE VISITORS

Figure out your Moneyball Factor (see Chapter 3) to know how many site visitors you currently have and how many you will need to reach your goals.

Website Visitor Formula

Moneyball Factor x # of website visitors = # of car sales

Example: If you have a Moneyball Factor of 1 percent and 6,000 website visitors, you will sell roughly 60 cars. If the closing ratio stays the same and you double your traffic, you can sell 120 cars.
1 percent x 6,000 visitors = 60 car sales
1 percent x 12,000 visitors = 120 car sales

---

38 "Saying Good-bye to Commission-Based Car Sales," Matt Jones, Edmunds. com. Last Modified February 27, 2014, http://www.edmunds.com/car-buying/saying-good-bye-to-commission-based-car-sales.html.

If car dealers go in blindly without knowing the resources they need to sustain their car-selling mission, they could very well end up lost somewhere in the Automotive Bermuda Triangle. To create accurate, achievable sales goals and advertising budgets, continue monitoring the relationship between your inventory, personnel, and website visitors. See Chapter 22 for a real-world example of how understanding the Automotive Bermuda Triangle can make it easier for you to become a Car Dog Millionaire.

CHAPTER 10 SUMMARY

Answer: D, Bermuda Triangle

Key Point: After five US Navy Avenger airplanes disappeared without a trace in the Bermuda Triangle, no extraordinary evidence emerged to indicate that the casualties resulted from anything other than physical causes. Like this mythical area of the Atlantic, advertising budgets tend to also be a misunderstood space for car dealers. If dealerships go in blindly not knowing the supplies they need to sustain their car-selling mission, they could very well end up lost in the Automotive Bermuda Triangle. To set achievable, ambitious sales goals, triangulate the relationship between your inventory, personnel, and web visitors.

Summary:

- Shopping doesn't happen at the store.
- Sales tracking starts at your website.
- Online car transactions will happen someday.
- To avoid wasting your money and missing your sales goals, take the time to learn the Automotive Bermuda Triangle: the relationship between your personnel, inventory, and website visitors. Five minutes a month can make a huge difference.
    - Inventory Formula: # of cars on ground ÷ 2 = # of cars to sell (goal)
    - Personnel Formula: # of cars to sell ÷ 10 cars/person = # of salespeople needed

- Website Visitor Formula: Moneyball Factor x # website visitors = # of car sales
- Does it look like the numbers match up? If there's too much wish in any one of your sectors, you'll end up falling short of your sales goals.

Eleven

Drive Your Moneyball
Factor Forward

11. In baseball, what is the term for the fourth batter in a lineup?

A. Show

B. Cleanup

C. Designated Hitter

D. Babe

Considered one of the greatest hitters in baseball history, Theodore Samuel "Ted" Williams earned himself the nickname "Teddy Ballgame," and with good reason. In September of 1941, Williams's batting average stood at 0.39955 on the final day of the season.[39] His manager, Joe Cronin, checked with Major League Baseball (MLB) and confirmed that Ted's average would be rounded up to the next decimal place and offered Williams the option to sit out of the season-ending doubleheader in order to guarantee a 0.400 batting average.

Yet Williams chose to take his chances. Instead of sitting on the bench, he trusted in his skill and played ball. In the final two

---

39 "Ted Williams's .406 Is More Than a Number," B. Pennington, *The New York Times.* Last Modified September 17, 2011, http://www.nytimes.com/2011/09/18/sports/baseball/ted-williamss-406-average-is-more-than-a-number.html?pagewanted=all&_r=1.

games, he went 6 for 8 and finished the season with a 0.406 batting average—a record Williams still holds as the last MLB player to bat over 0.400 in a season. In the seventy plus years since, no other hitter has reached a batting average this high.

Teddy Ballgame's determination shows the power of following through despite already being near the top. When you choose not to rest but persevere, you can walk away with more than you ever thought possible.

MONEYBALL FACTORS

Like a batting average, a dealership's Moneyball Factor can function as a benchmark for business, as it provides a glimpse at the current relationship between its website, car sales, and profitability.

The Moneyball Factor = # of cars sold ÷ # of website visits

You may crunch the numbers and realize your dealership is already thriving in selling cars. If you get comfortable, take the day off, and take a seat on the bench, you may just open up the floor for your competitors to steal sales. Maximizing your return on investment means tracking your Internet dealership with frequency and continuing to push forward, even when you're already on top of your game like Teddy Ballgame.

Keep in mind, your Moneyball Factor is a simple performance indicator and provides an executive-level summary of how your dealership is performing. To really understand this number and how to improve it, you should step back and look at all of the factors that influence it. Like an MLB player, you need to think strategically about your strengths and weaknesses to devise a training plan.

To help our dealers think more specifically about their own strengths and weaknesses, we created a "Moneyball Lineup" of the top ten most influential factors to success. Much like the American League batting order, where you have nine position players and one designated hitter, I evaluated the impact of each factor and organized them like players in a batting order. The order of the list is just as significant as the numbers on each jersey, which represent the percentage of the dealership's budget that should be allocated to that area.

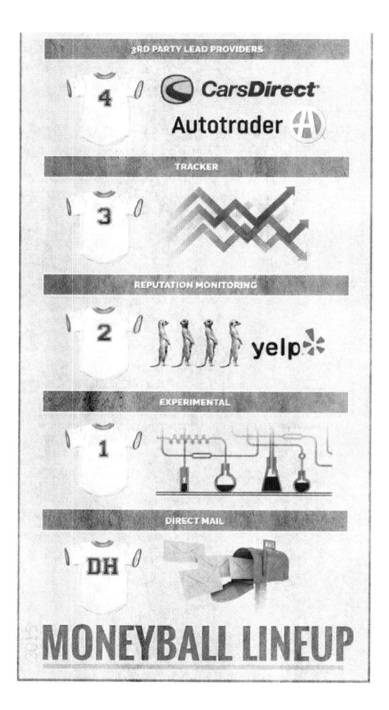

Budget 28 percent to the service drive and use a third-party call management service to handle all scheduling and calls. If you let someone else answer the simple questions like, "Are you open on the weekend?" or "Do you have this car part in stock?" then you allow your employees to focus their time on more meaningful tasks that will impact your dealership sales goals. Keith Shetterly and his team at AutoLoop help service advisers stay off the phone so that customers can get frequently asked questions answered through a call center that also helps to schedule service appointments.[40] As the most profitable department in the dealership, it takes common sense and makes financial sense to first prioritize your service drive.

Next up, budget 10 percent to building your website, creating SEO content, and installing a chat service to answer questions and maintain your presence online. Then put 20 percent behind search engines and prioritize Google, keeping Yahoo and Bing on your radar. Invest approximately 27 percent in cable TV and radio—which are expensive, yet still effective mediums to reach your audience. Be sure to understand how your advertising association and national spot markets contribute to this component. (See Chapter 2 for more details.)

For the rest of your budget, use 5 percent for social media, 4 percent for third-party lead providers, and 3 percent for a part-time person to track all of your dealerships stats and goal progress. Then, use 2 percent for reputation management software and set 1 percent aside for whatever new advertising medium appears to capture the next wave of digital buyers. Many years ago, this type of experimental budget was reserved for Facebook.

---

40 "Off the Phone, Shops Stay on the Job," L. Chappell, *Automotive News*. Last Modified October 5, 2015, http://www.autonews.com/article/20151005/RETAIL05/310059988/off-the-phone-shops-stay-on-the-job.

Today it might be better served for Periscope, Meerkat, Pinterest, or Instagram. Finally, reserve direct mail as your "designated hitter" and use it only at the end of the month if it will help you reach an objective, as it can be highly effective when delivered in the right amounts at the right time.

Now that you know how to allocate your budget, continue reading on to find out why money spent here will help make you a Car Dog Millionaire.

CHAPTER 11 SUMMARY

Answer: B, Cleanup

Key Point: In baseball, the fourth hitter generally has the most power on the team, as his job is to "clean up the bases." In the "Moneyball Lineup" for dealerships, the money you put behind radio and cable TV is very effective in marketing your dealership. Budget some of your advertising dollars here by determining how the really heavy hitters in your market—the OEMs and the advertising associations—are spending, and then spread the rest of your budget across the other areas to create a strong presence that will keep pushing your sales forward while maintaining a level eye toward driving profitable retail sales.

Summary:

- In 1941, Teddy Williams chose to stay in the game. A true competitor, Teddy Ballgame finished with a 0.406 batting average that has not since been equaled.
- Knowing your Moneyball Factor will give you a glimpse at your dealership's current performance in the market.
- Use the "Moneyball Lineup" batting order to guide your dealership's budgeting.
- Instead of slowing down when your dealership is at peak performance levels, keep pushing to understand the supporting factors that drive success.

Twelve

Make Meaningful Goals, Not Viral Ones

12. What color is the dress in this picture?

A. White and Gold
C. Black and Blue

B. Black and Beige
D. Yellow and Brown

If you happened to be on the Internet on February 25, 2015—or watched TV, listened to the radio, or talked to other people who did, you probably heard about this dress. The image took the world by storm for one reason and one reason only: people couldn't agree on the color of the dress.

Some clearly saw white and gold, while others swore on black and blue. After the photo went viral, Roman Originals—creator of the dress—confirmed the material as blue and black. So why did some people perceive it differently?

Luckily for the confused masses, reporters and intellectuals teamed up to take a stab at explaining the science behind this puzzling picture. Dan Diamond from *Forbes* broke it down this way: "It's because some of our brains are confused by the original image's washed-out, bluish lighting. Our visual systems intuitively know to filter out normal backgrounds and lighting in order to see the "true" color of an object—a concept called color constancy—but the bluish tint to the photo is throwing off that ability for many people," said Diamond.[41]

Adam Rogers from *Wired* met with neuroscientist Bevil Conway from Wellesley College to dig deeper into the phenomenon. "What's happening here is your visual system is looking at this thing, and you're trying to discount the chromatic bias of the daylight axis," Conway told Rogers. "So people either discount the blue side, in which case they end up seeing white and gold, or discount the gold side, in which case they end up with blue and black."[42]

No matter what color you see, the scientific explanation of the photo is as fascinating and perplexing as the speed at which it infiltrated the Internet. After Caitlin McNeill posted the photo on Tumblr, BuzzFeed publicized the debate and sparked a fire that rapidly spread around the world. The image captivated millions as they shared, blogged, and joined the conversation to weigh in on the great debate of colors. Even celebrities like Taylor Swift and Justin Bieber added their two cents on Twitter.

---

41 "Why Your Brain Thinks That Blue Dress Looks White," D. Diamond, *Forbes*. Last Modified February 27, 2015, http://www.forbes.com/sites/dandiamond/2015/02/27/the-science-behind-why-that-blue-dress-looks-white/.
42 "The Science of Why No One Agrees on the Color of This Dress," A. Rogers, *Wired*. February 26, 2015, http://www.wired.com/2015/02/science-one-agrees-color-dress.

Taylor Swift @taylorswift13 · Feb 26

I don't understand this odd dress debate and I feel like it's a trick somehow.
I'm confused and scared.
PS it's OBVIOUSLY BLUE AND BLACK

110K   166K

Justin Bieber ✔
@justinbieber

And for everyone asking I see blue and black

6:21 AM · 27 Feb 15

27,6K RETWEETS **32,7K** FAVORITES

Interestingly enough, this picture's organic spread reflects how Gen Yers and Gen Zers process information in the ever-connected world they live in. Perception is reality; when they do not understand something, they Google it. And when Google fails to provide a concrete answer, they join the masses and Tweet their opinions via social media. When things "go viral" in a matter of hours, it reminds us of—yet again—how powerful the Internet has become in connecting people.

Now companies and marketers alike are trying to dissect the curious case of what makes some images, stories, and videos go viral. While there are marketing lessons to be learned from the dress, setting goals to go viral is *not* how dealerships should be using the Internet to sell more cars.

Viral campaigns can disappear just as quickly as they arrive. One viral campaign, no matter how bold or brave, will not turn you into a Car Dog Millionaire. To get to an elite level of selling cars, you must put in the work overtime. Hire the right people, measure the right data, update your website, and analyze the traffic. Great marketing results from a series of deliberate, focused actions designed to help you improve. For car dealers, the ultimate goal is to create meaningful connections with customers. Leave it up to another dealership to catch a virus.

CHAPTER 12 SUMMARY

Answer: A or B, depending on the way your eyes perceive it.

Key Point: The colors of the dress appear white and gold or black and blue, depending on the human eye's system for filtering out background and lighting. The widespread reach of the viral image is fascinating, and while entertaining, it sets the stage to remind dealers of what *not* to do. Going viral like this image is not the goal for car dealerships. To consistently captivate and capture car shoppers, dealers must use the Internet and a more disciplined approach to build marketing metrics and sales performance in meaningful, consistent ways over time.

Summary:

- In February 2015, a picture of a dress made its way around the world because people couldn't decide on what color it was.
- Neuroscientists chimed in on the debate to confirm that the image of the dress appeared to be different colors depending on the way your eyes perceived it.
- The organic sharing of the image reflects the way Gen Yers and Zers process information over the Internet.
- Instead of trying to create viral campaigns like the dress picture, dealerships should be using their online presence to connect with consumers in more meaningful ways.

Thirteen

"It's Time to Make the Dough-nuts!" with Social Media

13. Which company used the catchphrase, "Time to make the donuts!"?

A. Shipley Do-Nuts   B. Van Tuyl Companies
C. Berkshire Hathaway   D. Dunkin' Donuts

Fred the Baker, played by Michael Vale, served as the popular character from Dunkin' Donuts commercials from 1981 to 1997. His catchphrase "Time to make the donuts!" spurred the growth of the Dunkin' franchise and garnered recognition as one of the five best commercials of the 1980s by the Television Advertising Bureau.[43] The message behind the spots appealed to Americana and drove home the point that Fred had to get up early every business day to make the doughnuts so that he could greet his customers with fresh new products.

---

43 "Dunkin' Donuts Press Kit," Dunkin' Donuts. Last Modified January 2015, http://news.dunkindonuts.com/internal_redirect/cms.ipressroom.com.s3.amazonaws.com/227/files/20153/Dunkin%20Donuts%20Press%20Kit%20-%20April%202015.pdf.

Are you making the donuts for your dealership with your social media? Sure you sell cars, but on a day-to-day basis one of the best ways to stay in front of your customers is through carefully considered social sites. You can make all the dough by executing on some of the plans detailed in the pages that follow. Not all at once, my friends…but consistently and relentlessly over time. "It's time to make the dough-nuts!"

Dealerships should connect through social media in order to stay relevant in today's economy. When companies create profiles and interact with consumers online, they build their brand, relationships, and reputation in the process. The more a company actively engages on social sites, the more control and influence it will have over its business perception as well as Google's Page One results.

For car dealerships, using social platforms in the right way will lead to more business, more leads, and more car sales. Social media includes all the websites and applications that allow users to interact, collaborate, create, and share content. If the purpose of the different social sites seems confusing, look no further than Urban Dictionary for some clarity—their definition of social media really nails it. "'Social Media: Your Electronic Second Life' can be best described using examples and the corresponding translations:

- Facebook: I like doughnuts.
- Twitter: I'm eating #doughnuts.
- Instagram: Here is a polaroid-esce photo of doughnuts.
- Foursquare: This is where I eat doughnuts.
- YouTube: Here I am eating doughnuts.
- MySpace: Meet the up-and-coming band Doughnuts.

- LinkedIn: My skills include doughnut eating.
- Pinterest: Here is a recipe for doughnuts.
- eHarmony-Review: David Doughnuts, round, sweet personality, loves Krispy Kreme.
- G+: I'm a Google employee who eats doughnuts.
- Tumblr-Explore tags: F**kyeah! Doughnuts!"[44]

As a brand, think about your products and services like doughnuts. Who do you want to show your doughnuts to? What audience might like seeing your goods? Once you figure out your target market, you can narrow down the priority networks you need to be on, which ones you can pass on, and how to effectively share on the ones you choose.

Going online as a car dealer might look something like this:

- Facebook: I like *cars.*
- Twitter: I'm selling #*cars.*
- Instagram: Here is a polaroid-esce photo of *cars.*
- YouTube: Here I am, selling *cars.*
- ...You get the idea.

To get your dealership name in front of people and start turning contacts into customers, you should be active on the following social sites. Once you make a profile on each site, keep in mind the golden rule of social: you must post, and you must listen. If you let your profile go dormant or ignore what people are saying about you, you will miss opportunities to do business and become a trusted resource.

---

44 "Social Media," Urban Dictionary. Last Modified February 6, 2012, http://www.urbandictionary.com/define.php?term=Social+Media.

GOOGLE+

When Google created this platform, it didn't quite gain traction as the one-stop social network they wanted it to be. Since launching in June 2011, Google+ has changed management three different times, operating under Vic Gundotra, then David Besbris, and now Google's VP Bradley Horowitz.[45] Despite Google's rank as the number-one place to work in the country, even the top guys there are struggling to deliver a successful outcome.[46]

As Horowitz takes the project under his wing, he plans to reorganize it into "Google's Photos and Streams Products" and tap further into the visual market. Stay tuned to the company's next phase of optimization to see if this third-time change of management will be the charm, or the ultimate demise of Google+ as we know it. According to *Wired* writer David Pierce, "Don't write the obituary yet...Google as a social network is very much alive."[47]

As Google+ goes through a transition, you want to stay ahead of the game for when/if they pull through. Go ahead and make your dealership a profile on Google +. Include all of your business contact information, and then do a Google Search Results review to see if your Google+ profile appears on the first or second results page. Keep an eye on the rank; it will give you an indication of what is coming soon: i.e., if Google+ starts edging up, your efforts on the platform should, too.

---

45 "The Head of Google+ Has Reportedly Quit His Job," R. McCormick, *The Verge*. Last Modified on March 2, 2015, http://www.theverge.com/2015/3/2/8131425/head-of-google-has-reportedly-quit-job.

46 "100 Best Companies to Work for in 2015," *Fortune*. Last Modified February 2015, http://fortune.com/best-companies/.

47 "Google+ as We Knew It Is Dead, but Google Is Still a Social Network," D. Pierce, *Wired*. Last Modified March 2, 2015, http://www.wired.com/2015/03/google-knew-dead-google-still-social-network/.

FACEBOOK

The importance of listening to what's being said online can't be underestimated on the world's most popular social medium. It's not so much that Facebook will sell you cars; it's that it can keep you from selling cars. Ideally, you want to create a profile to portray a personable, accurate image of your dealership and use it to connect with customers. Be sure to include stock photo pictures of some of your cars, along with a few short, instructional videos from your sales team on the lot. Set a goal to post about three to five times a week and share things like store promotions or positive reviews left on other sites.

At the start and end of every workday (no less than every twelve hours) have your marketing manager or ad agency check Facebook. You can also download Perch: an app for small businesses that sends push notifications when people post/interact with your profiles. This will help you respond in a crisis situation, if and when consumers have concerns.

TWITTER

Successful auto brands are building audiences on Twitter and using the platform to get consumers more excited than ever about their promotions and cars. On Twitter, the goal is to integrate yourself into the conversation. The worst thing to be is tone deaf. Be online to listen and respond to the people engaging with you. When you're in, be all in—much like you'd be at a cocktail party. Stay on topic and contribute to the conversation at the right times.

For your dealership's Twitter profile, hire someone either on your team or from an outside agency to manage it. Similar to Facebook, you can share dealership promotions, blogs, and articles from employees at your dealership, or links to important industry news. Feel free to also include pictures of customers test-driving vehicles and any Instagram photos from your dealership.

Don't post and run or rely on an auto-scheduler to tweet. Every time you post, hang around on the site to see where the conversation goes. Be willing to spend a few extra moments to search hashtags for your manufacturer and see what people are saying. Set a goal to write a meaningful tweet at least three times a week.

VIMEO

Video sites are a great place to create shareable content for your brand's story, deals, and promotions. If you create videos and optimize the content for search engines, you increase your chances of being found organically online. After you create a Vimeo account, you can upload any videos from your dealership or TV commercials for your store. These videos can be as simple as a two-minute interview with the service director about the best way for consumers to buy parts more efficiently: i.e., you could walk through how to find and fill out the online form and e-mail it to the dealership. Build a library over time with simple videos, and always insert SEO information on Vimeo. Shoot to post and share a new video at least one time a month.

PERISCOPE

To give customers a personal way to connect with everything happening at your dealership, check out Periscope or its Facebook-owned friend, Meerkat. The apps let you broadcast live video for free to communicate with the public in real time. While you are streaming, viewers can send messages to comment and ask questions, and you can address them while you are on the air. It can be used to build awareness for the brand (i.e., broadcasting videos live from your store), and it can also be leveraged as a relationship-building tool. Maybe you have a funny sales team member who wants to share car-buying tips in an entertaining way, or perhaps you want to host a webinar with service drive information.

Brainstorm creative ways to share your dealership's personality, expertise, and talent with the public. Then create an account on Periscope and start streaming, commenting, replying, and connecting with customers.

INSTAGRAM

Most things you would want to share on Instagram will happen at the dealership. Think of this platform as a way to share the personable and positive moments in your team's workday. When you create an Instagram account, don't pay an outside company to manage it for you. Delegate this task to an existing employee.

Post pictures to celebrate happy events: a new hire, an employee's one-year work anniversary, a new car model, a sales event, or a smiling customer leaving the lot with his or her new wheels. This is a medium whereby consumers can connect with your team on a human level.

LINKEDIN

LinkedIn is essentially Facebook for business professionals. According to the site's analytics, professionals are signing up to join LinkedIn at a rate of more than two new members per second.[48] Create a business page for your dealership, and send invitations to connect with previous customers to start building your follower base. If you are selling near-luxury to luxury cars (like Lexus, Acura, Infinity, Mercedes, BMW, or Audi), you better have a presence here, as the professionals using LinkedIn are in your target demographic to buy the cars from your lot. Use a portion of your advertising budget to market your dealership on the site, and set the parameters to ten to twenty miles around your dealership to cover your primary market area. The ad design can be simple: an image of your logo that links back to the dealership homepage.

Year-round advertising is recommended on LinkedIn, with the most important months being March, May, August, and December for those with more limited resources.

PINTEREST

In 2014, Pinterest began offering in-depth analytics for businesses which catapulted the platform to major player status in the social media game. During that year, Pinterest's referral traffic to main websites through pins grew by 48 percent.[49] By September 2015, Pinterest's user base surpassed 100 million users.[50]

The capabilities of the platform along with the analytics help engage consumers with your content. While Pinterest today is not about monetizing, it may be in the near future. If you haven't

---

48 "About Us," LinkedIn. Last Modified May 11, 2015, https://press.linkedin.com/about-linkedin.

49 "Facebook and Pinterest Are the King and Queen of Social Referrals [REPORT]," D. Wong, D., Shareaholic. Last Modified April 24, 2014, https://blog.shareaholic.com/social-media-traffic-trends-04-2014/.

50 "Reach 100 Million Interested People" Pinterest. Last Modified September 16, 2015, https://business.pinterest.com/en/blog/reach-100-million-interested-people.

already, it's time to get your piece of the Pinterest pie by building a subscriber base and pinning in your favorite categories.

Create industry-specific boards, like blogs worth reading or cars that catch your eye. Then electronically embrace your humanity and push yourself to go beyond business. Include parts of life and culture significant to your dealership. For example, if you are a dealer in Columbus, Ohio, you could create a board on "Chasing the Championship for Ohio State Football."

Take advantage of Pinterest Analytics, as they provide the number of clicks on a pin and impressions, insight into where your followers live, and topics that interest them. Use this information to tailor your content to optimize engagement and brand awareness for your makes, your models, and your market.

Try to create at least five boards for your dealership that make you intriguing and visually compelling to the community. After the initial five, create a new board for every calendar month. For instance, on a board for January 2016, pin pictures of all the people who bought cars from your lot that month. This will create a visual, dynamic history of your happy customers. Try the same thing for February 2016 and then March 2016. Wash. Rinse. Repeat.

If you want to win the Pinterest game, stay consistent every month and create new boards. To make this happen, first institute a process for how the salesperson will take pictures after he or she completes a sale. Get customer consent by having them sign a waiver (below). Then the salesperson can snap a quick picture on his or her iPhone and text it to the social media manager at the dealership or agency, who will then pin it to the right folder.

TALENT RELEASE AGREEMENT

For valuable consideration, the sufficiency and receipt of which is hereby acknowledged, I, the undersigned, agree as follows:

I consent to the use of my name, voice, image, likeness, and any and all attributes of my personality, in, on, or in connection with any film, audio tape, audio-visual work, photograph, illustration, animation, or broadcast, in any media or embodiment, now known or unknown, including, without limitation, all formats of computer readable media, produced by or for the benefit of _____. I further consent to the use of my name, voice, image, likeness, and any and all attributes of my personality in any advertising or promotional material created or used in connection with _____, and each such item of advertising or promotional material will be considered a "Work" for purposes of this agreement.

I irrevocably assign to _____ (a) any and all claims of copyright I may have in and to _____, and (b) the exclusive and perpetual right throughout the world to use, print, produce, publish, copy, display, perform, exhibit, transmit, broadcast, disseminate, market, advertise, sell, lease, license, transfer, modify, and create derivative works from _____ in any media or format, now known or unknown, for any purpose whatsoever.

I waive any right to inspect or approve the content of _____.

I agree that _____ will have no obligation to utilize the authorizations and rights I grant to _____ hereunder.

I hereby release, discharge, and agree to hold harmless _____, its legal representatives and assigns, all persons acting under its authority, and those for whom it is acting, from all claims, cause of action, and liability of any kind, now known or unknown, in law or in equity, based upon or arising out of _____ or this agreement including, without limitation, claims of libel, slander, invasion of privacy, right of publicity, defamation, trademark infringement, and copyright infringement.

I represent and warrant that I am over the age of eighteen (18) years, and that the authorizations and rights granted hereunder do not conflict with or violate the rights of any third party.

This agreement will be binding upon my heirs, successors, representatives, and assigns.

Date: _____

Signature:_____

Name: _____

Ph.#: _____

On the Internet, the wisdom of the masses reigns supreme. Seize the opportunity! Engage on social sites and show the world your #doughnuts—and all the other things your dealership is made of. When your online presence is rich with thoughtful commentary, happy employees, satisfied customers, and killer sales events, you will be well on your way to becoming a Car Dog Millionaire.

CHAPTER 13 SUMMARY

Answer: D, Dunkin' Donuts

Key Point: Dealerships should be reaching out to make personal connections with the people they depend on: their customers. Today, the best way to do that is through social media.

Summary: The more a company actively engages on social sites, the more control and influence it will have over their business's perception. Dealerships should know how to use and have a presence on the following sites:

- Google +
  - Post here to help your organic search rankings and keep your eye on the platform to see how it progresses.
- Facebook
  - Create a professional business page and include dealership information, car pictures, promos, videos, and anything else to make it another compelling way to reach customers.
- Twitter
  - Join the conversation on a national and local level by posting three meaningful tweets each week and hanging around on the site for twenty minutes after to reply and engage.
- Vimeo
  - Film helpful videos to answer popular FAQs the dealership gets and also post any TV commercials here.

- Periscope
  - Join the live streaming site and use this as a way to generate brand awareness and build relationships.
- Instagram
  - Take photos and share images of the personal side of your dealership team.
- LinkedIn
  - Create a company page and if you are selling near-luxury to luxury cars, allocate a portion of your advertising budget here.
- Pinterest
  - Use this site creatively to build boards of happy customers and location-related interests.

Fourteen

Use the Internet to Sell Cars Like a Champion

14. According to the *Guinness Book of World Records,* who earned the title of being the "World's Greatest Retail Salesman"?

A. Joe Girard

B. Zig Ziglar

C. Jim Ziegler

D. David Kain

Growing up in a ghetto on the east side of Detroit, Michigan, Joe Girard started working his first job at the age of nine as a shoe-shine boy in the neighborhood bars. With a poor and bitter immigrant father and a positive, supportive mother, Girard spent his earliest years trying to earn money for his family and escape his father's anger. He worked various jobs, dropped out of school by eleventh grade, and joined the army infantry by eighteen. It wasn't until years later when he hit an all-time low that he found something that would forever change the course of his life: selling cars.

Unemployed, in debt, and facing his own hungry family, Girard begged a sales manager at a Chevrolet dealership for a job. He sold his first car the day he got hired and eighteen cars during his second month there. Soon the other salespeople complained about his aggressive selling, so the owner fired him. But by then, Girard had already discovered his knack for selling cars. He went on over to work for another Chevrolet dealership in Eastpointe, Michigan, where he set a record selling 1,425 new cars in one year.[51] For twelve consecutive years, Girard held the title from the *Guinness Book of World Records* as the "World's Greatest Retail Salesman" for selling more "big ticket" items "one at a time" than any other salesperson in the entire retail industry.[52] During his fifteen years in retail, he sold 13,001 automobiles total.[53]

While Girard used his drive, strong work ethic, and people skills to sell cars, specialization became a vital key to his incredible track record of success. After his third year in the business, he focused on selling and hired someone else to do the prequalifying and screening process for him. No longer bogged down with paperwork, Girard sold more cars with less effort. A few months later, he decided to hire another person to help grow his business. By strategically allocating his time to his strengths and investing money in people to take on the rest, he built and sustained himself as a car-selling legend.

Though investing in people with the right skill sets remains valuable in running an efficient dealership today, the car industry has evolved since Girard's glory days in the 1960s and 1970s. Now

51 Wilson, Amy. "Joe Girard, A Man for the Record Books, Sold 13,001 Chevrolets in 15 Years." Automotive News. October 31, 2011. Accessed November 23, 2015. http://www.autonews.com/article/20111031/CHEVY100/310319926/joe-girard-a-man-for-the-record-books-sold-13001-chevrolets-in-15.

52 Joe Girard. (2015). *The History of Joe Girard*. Retrieved September 8, 2015, from Joe Girard: http://www.joegirard.com/biography/. Also see Parsons, O.J. "There's Nothing Humble about Joe Girard." *Spokesman-Review*, October 27, 1981, Today/Trends sec.

53 Ibid.

the real secret to selling cars like a Car Dog Millionaire requires more than just manpower to excel—it requires the Internet.

With car shoppers conducting their research online, your selling strategy should start there, too. Focus 80 percent or more of your marketing efforts on retail, and make it as easy as possible for consumers to find your dealership, inventory, and specials online. Use the following six components to strengthen your digital selling strategy and bring shoppers from the computer to the dealership.

INVENTORY SEARCH

When consumers shop online for cars, you want them to find *all* the vehicles on your lot. If you are a Ford dealer, you may have other makes for sale in your used car inventory. To make sure shoppers see all your vehicles when browsing online, you need to understand the unique differences between search engine optimization (SEO) and search engine marketing (SEM), and when to apply each tactic properly.

> SEO: *These are strategies to make a website accessible to search engines and increase the chances that it will be found through organic search. It's the marathon part of the business.*
>
> SEM: *This is a broader term that encompasses all the ways a business can use search engine technology to increase its website visibility, including paid listings and other services that help position a website within targeted search results. This is the sprint part of the business.*

Consumers starting their car shopping online may start with a very broad search like "minivan." As they get more involved in researching, their searches become more sophisticated with extended keywords like "2015 Honda Odyssey EX-L." A Honda dealership with strong SEO has a good chance of appearing for this Google search, as a large majority of their site features content about "Hondas." Yet a Ford dealer in the area that also has a 2015 Honda Odyssey EX-L in its used-car inventory might not even show in the results. Why?

Google indexes content roughly every day for its organic search results. Their process is algorithmic based on a number of factors that can speed up or slow down the frequency. For car dealers with transitory units like used cars that will ideally be on their site for less than sixty days, SEO alone will not give them the visibility they want during this time period. Instead, their inventory would be better served with SEM tactics via unique URL strings.

A **unique URL string** is a specific web address that is accessible on the Internet.

Example: http://www.fosterford.com/auto/used-2014-honda-odyessy-exl-alpharetta-30023-ga/3252234/

When you create a unique URL string like the example above, you can include the full car make, model, and year, as well as your dealership's location. The information provided in your unique URL assists search engines as they crawl the web to pull results for queries. Taking the time to set up accurate URLs will take you from being invisible in inventory searches to being right in front of the consumer.

KEYS FOR CREATING UNIQUE URL STRINGS

1. **List your city correctly:** If you are located outside a major metro market, do not list your dealership as inside that market in your URL strings. For instance, if you are in Alpharetta, then list your city as Alpharetta (not Atlanta). Though you are in a northern suburb of Atlanta, people want dealerships in close proximity to where they are searching or where they live. Stay true to your location to develop organic credibility with Google and your customers.

2. **Avoid acronyms:** Search engines use direct words from search queries to pull sources from the web. Thus, if you shorten coupe and sedan to CPE and SDN in your URLs, they will not appear in the corresponding online search results.

3. **Say "used car" instead of "preowned":** Though some dealers like the sound of *preowned cars*, consumers look for *used cars*. If you try to change the category name, you will make yourself accidently invisible, as search engines don't provide much traction for words and queries that aren't often used.

CHAT—HELLO!

As car shoppers shift to browsing dealership inventory online, you need to find a way to engage and communicate with them. Installing chat on your website allows you to greet customers directly, much like you would when they walk into the dealership.

It also takes the mystery out of the traffic numbers by letting the dealership ask and answer questions to find out more about each visitor and to help that visitor find what he or she is looking for in your virtual, online dealership.

Each month, you can initiate anywhere from 200 to 1,000 extra conversations through live chat, depending on the traffic to your site. If you manage to close 10 percent of those leads, imagine what that will do to your revenue stream.

JIM: *Hey, Car Dogs, grab those incremental sales!*

In the car industry, the cost of getting leads by using a chat service is relatively low compared to the revenue those leads can generate. By extracting contact information and scheduling appointments, you can build positive touch points with potential car buyers. Of course, the only thing worse than not having chat is having chat and not having anyone responding in a timely fashion with the right information. To avoid this, train your team before you sign your dealership up.

DEALER WEBSITE CHAT 101

1. **Open with a warm hello and introduce yourself.**

CHAT CONSULTANT: *Hi there, welcome to Texas Trucks. My name is Jessica; let me know how I can help you.*

2. **Create a list of frequently asked questions and answers.** You can anticipate the majority of questions consumers will ask. Write out the answers and instruct your sales team when to use these automatic responses. After

a chat comes in, set the goal to answer in five seconds or less.

CAR SHOPPER: *Do you still have this car on your lot?*
CHAT CONSULTANT: *Yes, all the available units we have on our site are on the lot.*

When your units online are updated daily, your chat consultant's job is not to find the unit at your dealership. No one wants to wait thirty seconds or more for them to locate the webpage or even longer for someone to run out on the lot to physically check. To get your team familiar with inventory as it changes, have the sales team members print out a list of units available on the lot each morning. Hard copy information flows faster than most dealer websites. Speed wins.

CAR SHOPPER: *What's the selling price?*
CHAT CONSULTANT: *The range is $22,000 to $26,290 on that particular model, and you should know that we don't lose deals based on price.*

Though this is a hypersensitive topic, you can't ignore talking about the price. Don't avoid the question—give them an honest answer with an accurate range.

CAR SHOPPER: *So how can I get a deal on this?*
CHAT CONSULTANT: *We offer a few discounts (i.e., loyalty and military), which you may qualify for. Can I find out more about you so I can give you the lowest price possible?*

People look for deals when buying cars and want to know how they can get to an advantageous position. Your goal is not to reshape thinking or try to change buying behavior. Instead, put the control in the consumer's hands and be on his or her side.

3. **Answer questions directly.** If the consumer asks a question that your team did not make a premade answer to, do not copy and paste one that is *close* to the question. Your job is to take the time and really answer it. As David Kain from Kain Automotive believes, chat involves a "Five minutes and Forever" moment.[54] If you take the five minutes to answer their questions, you can foster a forever relationship. Likewise, if you fail to do just that in those five minutes, the customers are gone forever.

4. **Familiarize yourself with the chat platform analytics.** Take a look at how the platform you use tracks each unique visitor and the pages they view. This will give you some extra information on their buying needs and interests. You can typically also see the number of times they visited your website, which can help you determine where they might be in the buying cycle.

5. **Monitor chats and give feedback.** To ensure quality control, monitor all the conversations going on to praise great communication and to coach your BDC team in areas that need work. To do this effectively, enable your platform to send a transcribed e-mail immediately to the sales management team. Assign someone on your team to be the

---

54 "Internet Sales 4.0: Secrets of a Successful Automotive Internet Operation," D. Kain, SlideShare. Last Modified October 24, 2011, http://www.slideshare.net/bikekain/cp0420grouppresentationdavidkain2011.

one-minute manager for chat. This person will read the chat as soon as it enters his or her inbox and will send instant feedback. Receiving honest feedback in the moment will motivate consultants to continue improving their chat skills. Car Dog Millionaires inspect what they expect.

SPECIALS UPDATES

As consumers browse around online looking for the best deals, the "Specials" page on a dealership website tends to attract a lot of traffic. Interestingly, these pages also have a very high bounce rate. If a consumer visits and does not see any deals, they leave.

When used correctly, the "Specials" page can help dealers maximize their potential to sell cars. Even so, it is habitually underutilized. Some dealers fear making deals too good and sacrificing their profitability, instead of thinking about it from a customer point of view. For example, when the Cash for Clunkers program started, many dealers were slow to participate as they feared they might lose money if they put out a deal better than the competition. As long as dealers fear profit sacrifices, they fear success.

Offering deals means giving consumers a reason to choose your dealership over the one down the road. Plus, when you track coupon redemption, you can connect your online efforts with offline consumer behavior. When one deal expires, cycle the next through. Strengthen your retail strategy and stay in the game by including specials on your website in these four categories:

1. **New Car Specials:** These should be up on your site each and every day of the month. When you offer incentives for people to buy new cars from your lot, you create a sense

of urgency with reason. Keep these deals fresh, and add new ones as the old ones expire.

2. **Used Car Specials:** Display used car specials and get car shoppers excited about the make, model, and deal. With the typical used car shelf life being sixty days or less, stay on top of cycling in new deals as the old cars sell.

3. **Service Drive Coupons:** Include time-sensitive coupons for your service drive to reach consumers in your market territory. Though some people worry about giving coupons to people who already buy from them, coupons create an incentive for consumers to choose you over competitors. Also keep in mind that a new car sells the first car, while service sells the next car.

4. **Parts Offers:** Include a very generic parts offer (i.e., a 5 percent off or 10 percent off parts orders greater than $200). Though many people prefer to leave the part buying and car fixing to the experts, extend the offer for the DIY guys and gals near your dealership.

Buy a Truck, Get a Gun Special
In May 2015, the Benny Boyd dealership group in Texas created a promotion to buy a truck and get a free gun. Talk about a creative special, given their market!

AUTO ALERTS
Getting a car to your service drive creates not only service business but also a potential trade unit that could end up in your used-car inventory. To better understand the business potential with the cars coming into your dealership, you need expertise from an equity mining company. Through statistical analysis,

these companies track the customer and car data at your service drive to find patterns and relationships.

Once you start using a tracking system, set up a program like Auto Alerts so that an assigned dealership employee can receive reports on the car history for each customer as they come in. This is an excellent yet undervalued way to move service customers into new car customers. Take advantage of it, as today's car fleet in the United States is one of the oldest on record.

MOBILE TEXT AND TRAFFIC

Keeping in mind that there are almost as many cell phone subscriptions as there are people on this Earth, mobile phones connect people in ways no other medium can. From anywhere in the world, you can send a message to a device that will reach the right person in the right moment.

The Lithia Auto Group recognized the potential with cell phones, and in April 2011, they decided to text people to deliver the following retail message: "0 percent financing on used vehicles during the biggest sale ever. Over 3,000 used vehicles at Lithia Motors."[55] They reached 57,800 consumers' phones and followed up the next week with another retail message that went out to 48,000 phones. Sure enough, a $2.5 million lawsuit and cautionary tale followed: learn the laws of new media before you blast retail messages.

The FCC bans text messages sent to a mobile phone using an auto-dialer unless you previously gave consent to receive the

---

55 "Lithia Faces $2.5 Million Tab for Texting," A. Sawyers, *Automotive News*. Last Modified December 19, 2011, http://www.autonews.com/article/20111219/RETAIL07/312199993/lithia-faces-$2.5-million-tab-for-texting.

message or the message is sent for emergency purposes.[56] While dealerships should steer clear of making the same mistake Lithia Auto Group did, there are more personal ways to get in touch with consumers via cell phone.

To abide by the FCC and Telephone Consumer Protection Act rules, you need a signed document that says they permit you to text them. This permission is especially useful for cars on the service drive. If your dealership needs to do a break repair, you can text the customer with pictures of the car, the service you recommend, and the price. This use of texting keeps things quick, personal, visual, and efficient.

To consent to text messages from the dealership, consumers must opt in to receive these SMS messages. Some companies now are trying to use a double-opt-in format (i.e., getting a customer's number and verbal consent, then texting to ask them to reply YES to receiving messages). From a commonsense standpoint, this seems like consent. Yet the law says you need a signed document to verify that they did opt in. Under the law, a signed napkin from a bar is more legally viable than a double-opt-in text approval. Here's why. With double opt in, someone could have borrowed your phone: your children, your spouse, your neighbor, or worse yet, a savvy Gen Y F&I director. Got it? Good!

If you want to eliminate all doubt, a simple document that says, "I opt in to receive text messages from 'your company name,'" is the best way to go. It may be just one more piece of paper to put in the F&I packet, but it could save you millions of dollars. Also remember, once you get that consent, always reserve text

---

56 "Spam: Unwanted Text Messages and Email," Federal Communications Commission, FCC.gov. Last Modified December 31, 2014, https://www.fcc.gov/guides/spam-unwanted-text-messages-and-email.

messages for personalized messages relevant to the consumer and his or her vehicle. If it feels like a mass blast, don't do it.

MOBILE APPS

Another valuable way to use mobile phones for your retail strategy is to offer mobile apps for your customers. When you give consumers the option to schedule services online or through their phone, you add convenience for all parties involved.

Consider using a service like the Xtime app for scheduling. Initially, the app will be a bit intensive to set up as it requires that you input the average times for your dealership's services (i.e., oil changes and repair orders for things like fixing breaks and installing new transmissions). Once you do this, you enable the platform to help consumer expectation meet reality with accurate scheduling times.

Additionally, when people can set an appointment with an automated scheduler, you do not need a service adviser taking the time to pick up the phone. One word of caution: do not accept appointments without being prepared to do business. If Saturday morning rolls around and you have seventy-five people trying to get oil changes with only three bays, you will see a lot of angry people. Been there. Done that. Not worth it. Avoid this by taking time in the beginning to set your dealership up for success at the service drive. To get your share of wallet, you first need to get your share of phone through a convenient, carefully considered mobile app.

CHAPTER 14 SUMMARY

Answer: A, Joe Girard

Key Point: Once Joe Girard discovered his talent for selling, he strategically allocated his time to this and invested money in people to take care of the rest. Using this team specialization, he established himself as a car-selling legend. Today, selling strategy is not just what happens on foot at the dealership; it starts from the moment consumers start browsing around online.

Summary: To transform your selling strategy into one of a Car Dog Millionaire, use the following components to bring shoppers from the computer to your dealership:
- Inventory Search
  - Make sure all the vehicles on your lot are visible online by creating unique URL strings that include vital dealership and car information.
- Chat
  - Install a chat service on your website and train your staff to initiate conversation, answer questions, and create an ideal shopping experience.
- Specials Updates
  - Keep your website fresh with car updates, as offering deals means giving consumers a reason to choose your dealership over the others.
- Auto Alerts
  - Use an equity mining company to receive car history reports on all the customers who come through your

service drive to alert your team when they are ready for a new car.

- Mobile Texting
  - Download a text consent form and only send personalized messages relevant to the customer and their vehicle.
- Mobile Apps
  - Connect your dealership with the Xtime app to make appointment scheduling easy for customers.

Fifteen

Reputation Management from Gen Y Perspective

15. Who said, "The most important yardstick of your success will be how you treat other people—your family, friends, and coworkers, and even strangers you meet along the way"?

A. Alan Mullaly

B. Mary Barra

C. Barbara Bush

D. Steve Jobs

Meet Christina, a twenty-something woman living in the suburbs of Chicago. Now a young professional with sustainable income, she wants to upgrade her car. She loves the look of the A7 Audi and jumps on a computer to look into it. She starts her research with a quick Google search for Audi dealers near her home with the query: "Audi Dealers Tinley Park."

Audi Dealer - Tinley Park - OrlandParkAudi.com
Ad www.orlandparkaudi.com/ ▾
Browse Our Online Audi Inventory Call For Latest Offers & Promotions

Audi Dealer Reviews - Find Top Audi Dealers
Ad www.dealerrater.com/ ▾
Read Reviews From Trusted Sources.
Cars for Sale - Dealer Reviews - Auto Service Reviews - Write a Review

Audi of Orland Park - DealerRater.com
www.dealerrater.com/dealer/Audi-of-Orland-Park-review-37... ▾ Dealer Rater ▾
★★★★★ Rating: 4.8 - 146 reviews
146 Reviews of Audi of Orland Park - Audi, Service Center Car Dealer Reviews &
Helpful Consumer Information about this Audi, Service Center dealership ...

Audi of Orland Park - Car Dealers - Tinley Park, IL - Reviews ...
www.yelp.com › Automotive › Car Dealers ▾ Yelp ▾
★★☆☆☆ Rating: 2 - 10 reviews
10 Reviews of Audi of Orland Park "My car has only been to this service department
and I cannot say enough praises on how I have been treated. I am greeted ...

Looks like there is an Audi Dealer close by albeit with mixed
reviews: 4.8 stars for DealerRater and only 2 stars for Yelp. Yikes.
Not familiar with DealerRater, she heads to Yelp first, as she already uses the site and trusts the wisdom of the masses there. The Yelp user reviews provide serious enough red flags so she decides not to waste her time and avoids this place.

 11/28/2014

Called the Finance Manager Today a 15+ year employee,
told him I just bought a used Audi and wanted an
extended Coverage plan. He told me I was in luck
because he had the at a discounted price this month of
November. He also told me His Audi dealership was the
ONLY one in the Chicagoland Area that sold an actual
Audi Pure Protection, all the other dealerships sell a 3rd
party protection. A LIE! I called Audi and EVERY
Chicagoland dealership and they ALL sell this plan. Not
only did I find an Honest Finance manager at another
dealership I also got the same plan $500 cheaper than his
sale price. The Business practice here is Unethical.
I'm sure I'm not the only person he has Lied to.
Do business here at your own risk.

Recognizing the bad reviews all came from the year prior, Christina decides to check out DealerRater to see what positive things people have to say. While browsing the reviews, she sees an ad for another Audi dealership and clicks through.

She lands at the Morton Grove Audi website a bit perplexed because she clicked on a "McGrath Audi" ad. She Googles this dealership, and it looks like McGrath changed their name to Morton Grove and moved locations. On Google, Morton Grove shows an average of 3.6 star reviews and on Yelp 3.5, with some really good reviews and some really bad ones.

Christina looks on the map and realizes the new location is north of the city, which is farther than she wants to drive from her house in the southern suburbs of Chicago. Not satisfied with any of the dealerships so far, she decides to head back to Google.

She figures the Chicagoland area is bound to have more dealerships, so she might as well broaden her parameters to see if a more ethical dealership exists. This time she searches "Audi Dealers Chicago."

Fletcher Jones Audi
fjaudi.com
4.5 ★★★★☆ 261 Google reviews · Google+ page

Ⓐ 1111 N Clark St
Chicago, IL
(312) 324-0884

Audi Morton Grove
audimortongrove.com
3.6 ★★★☆☆ 43 Google reviews · Google+ page

Ⓑ 7000 Golf Rd
Morton Grove, IL
(847) 998-8000

Audi Westmont
audiwestmont.com
4.5 ★★★★☆ 98 Google reviews · Google+ page

Ⓒ 276 Ogden Ave
Westmont, IL
(630) 537-0310

Map results for audi dealerships chicago

Wow! Check out Fletcher Jones with 261 Google reviews and a ranking of 4.5 stars. She pulls them up on Yelp and sees they have 185 reviews and 4 stars. She keeps reading to find an overwhelming number of authentic, positive reviews. Better yet, it looks like the dealership is personally addressing every negative review.

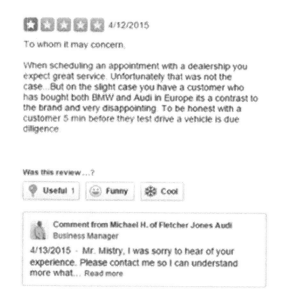

Now this is a dealership she feels good about visiting. While it is located about forty-five minutes away as opposed to ten minutes away for the other Audi dealership closer to her home, Christina is willing to drive a little bit farther to shop at a place that other people trust. If the masses say something is good, it usually is. So she runs with it.

A week later, she's the new owner of an Audi A7 and drives away as another happy customer raving about her experience at Fletcher Jones. She leaves a positive review as well because the dealership simply asked her to do so and she genuinely had a good experience.

THE POWER OF REVIEWS

Unlike a cocktail party, where gossip and stories get mixed among a small circle of friends and acquaintances, the Internet hosts review sites that blast comments for all the public to see. And these days, people have a lot to say. According to Domo's 2015 research on data generation, every minute Twitter users tweet 347,222 times, Facebook users like 4,166,667 pieces of content, and YouTube users upload 300 hours of new video.[57]

If consumers are saying good things about your brand, your positive reputation online will translate to more foot traffic at the dealership. On the other hand, a bad experience broadcasted for the world to see is one of the quickest ways to get the general public to lose faith and interest in your store. In today's world where people are visiting less than two stores on average before buying, managing brand perceptions about your dealership on the Internet is critical to car sales.

---

57 "Data Never Sleeps 3.0," J. James, Domo. Last Modified August 13, 2015, https://www.domo.com/blog/2015/08/data-never-sleeps-3-0/.

To build trust online, businesses need good reviews and they need a large quantity of them to legitimize their services. According to the 2014 WA Gallup survey, car salespeople are still one of the least trusted professionals in the country, with 45 percent of Americans rating them as having "very low" or "low" standards of honesty and ethics.[58] Hey, perception is unfortunately reality.

Here's the good news: no matter what kind of reviews are already floating around online about your dealership, you can change your reputation. Online reviews *are* in your control. Instead of passively listening to what people might be saying about your dealership, you can and should take a more active approach that starts with leading your dealership differently than you did before. To manage your reputation like a pro, you must learn from the experts.

INSIDER TIPS ON REPUTATION MANAGEMENT

In the glass corner office at the Mercedes-Benz of Chicago dealership sits the director of sales, Michael Halloran. Since making his first website for a Lexus dealership in 1999, Halloran has been working in the automotive digital space. Now he oversees marketing for the entire Fletcher Jones group—including their Audi, Honda, Mercedes-Benz, and Volkswagen dealerships. Remember the dealership with incredible reviews where Christina bought her new Audi? Halloran is the man behind their brand management.

After a few Google searches on the Fletcher Jones group, a striking similarity emerges among their stores. Each store features an abundance of positive reviews.

---

58 "Americans Rate Nurses Highest on Honesty, Ethical Standards," R. Riffkin, Gallup. Last Modified December 18, 2014, http://www.gallup.com/poll/180260/americans-rate-nurses-highest-honesty-ethical-standards.aspx.

Fletcher Jones Audi ☆

4.5 ★ ★ ★ ★ ★ 260 Google reviews
Audi Dealer

Fletcher Jones Honda ☆

4.2 ★ ★ ★ ★ 236 Google reviews
Honda Dealer

Mercedes-Benz of Chicago ☆

4.7 ★ ★ ★ ★ ★ 180 Google reviews
Mercedes-Benz Dealer

Fletcher Jones Volkswagen ☆

4.5 ★ ★ ★ ★ ★ 214 Google reviews
Volkswagen Dealer

Achieving this level of involvement and positivity in the automotive community does not happen by chance. Rather, it takes time and an analytical eye to understand the essence of building a strong brand—something the Fletcher Jones leadership team has developed. Continually cracking the code, they are a leader in solving the customer side of the marketing puzzle.

According to Halloran, customer satisfaction extends much deeper than how you sell the vehicles on the lot. "When you take away the cars, this business is about people," Halloran says. "Really, there are no shortcuts to reputation management. It starts at the core of your business with how you treat everyone that walks into your dealership."

He's not just talking about customers. Ever since Harry Gordon Selfridge famously said in 1909, *"The customer is always right,"* companies have been falling victim to management that values customers over employees.

Once employees start to feel undervalued or underappreciated, a divide transpires in the workplace. If the employees are unhappy, they will reflect it in their efforts and interactions. To put it simply, unhappy employees make for unhappy customers.

Halloran believes the secret to creating a respected brand starts with how you build relationships with *everyone*. "Train your salespeople to treat every person like they are a guest in your house. And treat your employees just as good as your customers."

A dealer's leadership team sets the precedent for company culture and can create an environment where employees feel respected, appreciated, and happy. As customers walk into the store, they can sense if camaraderie exists between employees. If it does, customers will feel more comfortable right off the bat.

Theoretically, the more positive interactions that happen at the dealership, the more positive online reviews the dealership should get—right? Unfortunately, the process is not that simple *yet*. Other variables like convenience and motivation influence whether or not a customer will leave a review. To take back control in this part of the process, some companies have tried to incentivize people to leave reviews. But paying the way to a better reputation might be too good to be true.

At first, giving monetary compensation to employees who get reviews for your dealership seems like a good idea to motivate them. In reality, it often results in the salespeople putting too much pressure on a customer for a review, which can adversely impact a customer's overall experience. According to Halloran, "When a sales member is feeling stressed or has some external motivator, the customers can sense that."

In the people business of selling cars, you can't fake authenticity. Overemphasizing the importance of a review can end in the customer leaving a scripted, forced review. Or it may scare them away from leaving one at all.

Trying to incentivize—or as some may say "bribe"—your consumers to leave reviews also isn't the wisest idea either. Once people find out a company paid someone to leave a review, it discredits the rest of the reviews. Remember, people go to review sites to find out what people *really* think, not what a company *paid* them to think.

"To motivate people to leave good reviews, you need to take the salesperson out of the equation," Halloran says. If you build a better business from the inside out and make feedback easy to give, you can put the customer in the driver seat. Since brand building starts at the core, the Fletcher Jones Group runs their dealerships using a strategic organizational structure. To keep their sales on track, they divide the sales employees into groups of four to five people. Each group has a team leader who oversees their progress and interactions. This person, like a diligent manager at a restaurant, helps facilitate the shopping experience by meeting customers early on in the process.

Once a customer is ready to make a purchase or wrap up his or her visit, they depart from the sales member to go into a simple exit interview with the team leader, whom they had previously talked with during the early management meet and greet. Through tactful coaching, team leaders invite their guest—the customer—into a personable, open environment to share feedback on the sales member who helped them. During this meeting, the team leader will address any issues and prep customers for a final exit survey they will be receiving after they leave. To streamline the feedback process, the Fletcher Jones Group uses a third-party reputation management software to send out exit surveys. Once they give the customer the tools, the dealership lets technology take care of the rest.

According to Halloran, "The goal is to remove hurdles for your sales team."

Since the salesperson's job has already been finished at this point, the responsibility shifts to the consumer. Within twenty-four hours of exiting the dealership, the customer will receive a simple e-mail that asks only one question: "Are you completely satisfied with your experience at this dealership? Yes or No."

If customers clicks the large *Yes* button, they will be automatically redirected to leave a review on the site they found the dealership on (i.e., Yelp, DealerRater, Google, etc.) By sending them to a familiar platform, the dealership removes barriers and makes the process seamless for customers to leave reviews.

If they answer *No*, they will be taken to an internal survey that gets sent to key members of the leadership team on both the corporate and dealership level. From here, the dealership recognizes employees who create positive customer experiences and looks for patterns in negative feedback that need to be addressed with the team. "Most negative reviews happen when a customer has raised expectations that we didn't meet," says Halloran.

To vet reviews, the team at Fletcher Jones determines the validity and accuracy of each comment and even takes human emotion into consideration. Then on a more technical level, they use the software to manage all of their review sites and connect with customers, and can even track their competitors' reviews. "It's the single, most effective tool I've found for reputation management," Halloran reports.

After using the third-party platform for two years, the Fletcher Jones Group went from receiving fifteen to twenty reviews a month to thirty to forty. It looks like when you treat customers excellently and give them an easy way to voice their opinion, they do it.

TAKE CONTROL OF YOUR REPUTATION

To audit your dealership's online reputation, familiarize yourself with all the review sites that come up on the first page when your dealership name is Googled. Ideally, you want the most recent reviews of your dealership on each site to be positive. If you see a negative review, explore the website to find out what actions you should be taking to address it. Whether you choose to reach out privately or publicly, do not let a bad experience hang in the air. The information on review websites can directly influence many other consumers' opinions. For car shoppers, DealerRater and Yelp have become two trusted, powerful resources when choosing a dealership to visit. Master these sites to put your best foot forward.

DEALERRATER

Tune in to see what people are saying about your dealership on DealerRater. When you pay money to advertise with the site, they give you two weeks to address negative reviews one-on-one with the dissatisfied customer before the review gets published publicly. If the issue is resolved, the customer can edit their review. This is incredibly valuable—take advantage of this opportunity to mend customer relationships before an isolated incident becomes a public and published complaint.

Hopefully, your positive reviews on DealerRater will far outweigh the negative. Share happy customer feedback by posting a link on Facebook and acknowledging the employees who worked with these customers. To gauge how valuable DealerRater is to your reputation, Google your dealership name and scan to see if the site shows up on the first page of results. If it does, strive to make sure your score is 4.0 or higher. If it doesn't show up, worry less about it. Either way, be proactive about monitoring reviews on DealerRater by checking the site once a week.

YELP

On Yelp, anyone can leave a review—and millions of people do. However, not all reviews are displayed. The site uses an algorithm to ultimately decide what reviews to recommend and count toward the overall business rating. As a dealership, this means you can have a very happy customer who writes a stellar review with 5 stars and Yelp can completely disregard it. For business owners, the flaws in the Yelp algorithm can be very frustrating.

Be aware of how the Yelp system for filtering reviews can help or hurt your business, as the site won't be going away anytime soon. Do not pay for advertising here, as it is not related to the reviews on your dealership. Yelp will not give positive reviews on your business favorability over negative—no matter how much you pay.

To see all your Yelp reviews, visit your dealership page and scroll down to the bottom to see other reviews that are not currently recommended. If you find some positive reviews from previous customers, you can give these reviews visibility and help them index with Google by copying and pasting them into a page on your website with the link back to Yelp. You can delete negative reviews on your website, but with online reviews, you are up against other people's version of the truth. Get the positive moments out there to the best of your ability.

Respond to every negative review both publicly and privately. Keep the tone positive, acknowledge the person's concern, and move the conversation forward by giving him or her a contact number or e-mail address to get in touch. As a business concern, you want your prospective customers to see that you address and take care of issues. No one expects perfection, but people do like to see authenticity and effort.

Anytime traffic slows at your dealership, visit your Yelp page. Stay on the offense with proactive, positive communication. If you are on the East or West Coast, you may be visiting Yelp more frequently, as success and traction with the site is more pronounced in major metros like Los Angeles and New York than it is in the Midwest or South.

CHAPTER 15 SUMMARY

Answer: C, Barbara Bush

Key Point: Barbara Bush's quote, "The most important yardstick of your success will be how you treat other people—your family, friends, and coworkers, and even strangers you meet along the way," also holds true for Car Dogs going after their millionaire dreams. To get on top and stay on top in the industry, you need to show kindness and respect for *everyone*. Even customers who don't buy from you can leave reviews.

Summary: Customer reviews matter, yet how you treat people matters more. The reviews your business gets will be a direct reflection of the way people interact and perceive your business.

- More and more people are going public with their opinions about brands and sharing their experiences with businesses for better or for worse.
  - Consumers saying good things about your brand online will translate to more foot traffic at the dealership.
  - Bad experiences broadcasted for the world to see are one of the quickest ways to get the general public to lose faith in your store.
- Take advice from car marketing guru Michael Halloran:
  - Avoid falling victim to a management style that values customers over employees; treat your customers excellently and treat your employees just as good as your customers.

- Instead of incentivizing people to leave reviews, pay for a simple reputation management software program that makes it easy both for customers to leave feedback and for your employees to facilitate the process.
- Set a goal on DealerRater to get a score of 4.0 or higher, and when you get positive reviews, share them with your business's network on Facebook.
- Stay proactive on Yelp using positive communication to address customer concerns that are brought into the public eye.

Sixteen

Swim Lanes, Shark Tanks, and Mad Men

16. In the final episode of *Mad Men*, what product does Don Draper market?

A. Coca-Cola

B. Adidas

C. Ford

D. Chevrolet

In 1971, ad executives from Coca-Cola arranged a meeting in London to work on a new song for their commercials. Bill Backer, creative director on the account from McCann Erikson, got on a plane to meet Billy Davis, the brand's music director also on the account. Due to dense London fog, Backer's plane was forced to land in Shannon, Ireland. The airline instructed passengers to stay close by the airport in the event that the fog cleared. The following day, Backer saw very irate passengers at the airport café—furious about their accommodations. He watched as anger turned into laughter as people bonded over their shared experience. They exchanged stories over snacks and bottles of Coca-Cola, and right there in the airport café, inspiration for the commercial unfolded in front of Backer. "In that moment [I] saw a bottle of Coke in a whole new light...as more than a drink that refreshed a hundred million people a day in almost every corner of the globe. So [I] began to see the familiar words, 'Let's have a Coke,' as more than an invitation to pause for refreshment. They were actually a subtle way of saying, 'Let's keep each other company for a little while.'"[59]

From there, Backer worked with Davis to record a song that captured the way Coca-Cola so peacefully brought people together. They worked on the melody and lyrics to produce the radio commercial, "I'd Like to Buy the World a Coke." After radio stations started getting requests to play the commercial like it was a hit record, Coca-Cola decided to record a video advertisement, featuring people from all over the world singing the song together. As soon as the commercial was released in the US in 1971, it resonated so powerfully with viewers that Coca-Cola received more than 100,000 letters about it.[60] The commercial captured the essence of coming together and plucked the heart strings of consumers all over the world. It was *precisely* what the consumers wanted, and it became an iconic commercial in the history of advertising.

Years later, when Matthew Weiner wrote the final episode for his show, *Mad Men*, he said, "Why not end this show with the greatest commercial ever made?"[61] And so, they aired the 1971 Coca-Cola "Hilltop" commercial.

---

59 "The Making of 'I'd Like to Buy the World a Coke," T. Ryan, Coca-Cola, Last Modified January 1, 2012, http://www.coca-colacompany.com/stories/coke-lore-hilltop-story/.
60 Ibid.
61 "Mad Men Creator Matthew Weiner Explains Series Final, Character Surprises and What's Next," A. Lee, Hollywood Reporter. Last Modified May 20, 2015, http://www.hollywoodreporter.com/news/mad-men-series-finale-matthew-797302.

NAVIGATING MODERN MARKETING

Today, the intricacies of the Internet have made advertising inherently more complex. Instead of building a brand message and simply deciding on radio, print, or TV ad campaigns, marketers are now faced with endless advertising choices to reach consumers online. They must consider format, placement, platform, timing, targeting, device, tracking…and the list goes on. It seems the more money and resources a business is willing to invest in digital advertising, the more complex they can make it. According to data from DG MediaMind, the top advertisers' online ad campaigns are nearly *six* times as complex as the average.[62] As digitally savvy advertisers build their intricate webs online, businesses in other industries like automotive are trying to keep up.

To make sense of it all, Honda Motor Corp created their own analogy: "If the Internet were a pool, what would advertisers be?" After analyzing the Google algorithm for ad placement, they confidently declared, "Swimmers in swim lanes." The company believed if dealers and the factory placed bids for the same words, they would be competing and raising prices for each other's words without improving ad position. Like swimmers in a pool, the brand advised their Acura and Honda dealerships to stay in their own lanes and refrain from bidding on key phrases that the factory wanted to go all in on. They hoped to save money by reducing the number of online, real-time auctions between like-minded keyword competitors in Google Search Results. To deliver their findings, Honda released a carefully considered thirty-eight-page document outlining "Honda and Acura's Paid Search Recommendation" at the 2014 Honda Dealer Advertising

---

62 "Is Online Advertising Getting Too Complex?" K. Kaye, *Ad Age*. Last Modified November 1, 2013, http://adage.com/article/datadriven-marketing/online-advertising-complex/245070/.

Conference in Las Vegas.[63] To its credit, Honda made participation in the program completely optional.

Coincidence or not, Google released a white paper called "Settling the (Quality) Score" on the exact same day the Honda conference started: June 24, 2014.[64] Just when brands thought they might have had Google's algorithm all figured out, the search engine giant announced fundamental adjustments to the common understanding of how the algorithm operated. By addressing "Quality Score"—the metric that advertisers believed to be *the* integral component to ad placement—Google debunked the swim lane theory before dealerships could even legitimately act on it.

Google's white paper stated, "Think of the Quality Score reported in your AdWords account as warning lights in a car: something that alerts you to potential problems. This number shouldn't be the main focus of your account optimizations. Yes, it should align with your performance if you're doing the right things. But trying to use tricks or short-term solutions to force the number up isn't the way to go." The irony of the car reference wasn't lost on Honda dealers or their advertisers.

Rather than using Quality Score, Google highlighted the real time evaluations of expected click through rate, ad relevance, and landing page experience to determine ad placement.[65] Advertising on the site is not controlled like a freestyle swim race. It's more—if you will—like swimming in shark tank filled

---

63 "Honda Digital Ad Budget to Grow," D. Barkholz, *Automotive News.* Last Modified August 18, 2014, http://www.autonews.com/article/20140818/RETAIL03/140819914/honda-digital-ad-budget-to-grow.

64 "Google Releases AdWords Quality Score Primer Aimed At Dispelling Misconceptions," G. Marvin, Search Engine Land. Last Modified June 24, 2014, http://searchengineland.com/google-releases-adwords-quality-score-primer-aims-dispelling-misconceptions-194941.

65 "Settling the (Quality) Score," Google. Last Modified June 24, 2015, http://services.google.com/fh/files/misc/settling-the-quality-score-whitepaper-final.pdf.

with competitors. If advertisers wanted to jump in and emerge at the other end for all the world to see, they needed to buy their name and show the Internet their true, authentic self. If they chose not to—for fear of competing with their own brand—they were on a path to potentially be eaten alive by hungry competitors like other manufacturers, other dealers, and third-party lead providers.

"People are happier with their search results, including the ads, when those results are relevant. Advertisers are more successful when they show relevant ads, as they're more likely to see engagement. It's with this in mind that we factor the quality of your ads into our AdWords auction," stated the Google white paper report.

To help advertisers navigate the waters, Google advised on what matters most when it comes to ad quality. According to the search engine, advertisers should think about mobile targeting for the user's device, making sure their ads and landing pages match the user wants, and investing in coverage on relevant searches in areas where their ads have high relevance. For car dealers, Google's message came in loud and clear: *Please be who you are, and yes, you should buy your name.* It's who you are!

The white paper also stated the importance of other factors that influence ad quality, including geographic signals and non-exact query matches. For example, if someone searches, "Honda dealership in Louisville," an ad for a dealership in Louisville would be more relevant than the Honda factory website—which factors into Google's ad rank. Therefore, the dealership and factory should invest in keywords that are true and relevant to each of them.

While the timely white paper makes Google seem a bit like an omniscient power, insiders from the automotive industry got wind of the "swim lane" announcement long before the Honda conference. Brian Pasch from PCG Consulting addressed the issue on his blog in March 2014, stating, "New buyers at any moment can move without prediction to buy a car. Tier 1 does not have a crystal ball to know when that will happen. The concept of restricting dealers to connect with shoppers seems like a step backward...the shopping path is uncontrolled; it's a free for all."[66]

As marketers and dealers tried to sort fact from fiction, they turned into a force of mad men all feverishly trying to nail down the secret behind ad ranking. Many believed the Quality Score metric shown in the advertiser's AdWord account factored into their placement. Yet the white paper addressed the integrated importance of Quality Score in ad ranking. A user's entire experience on a website meant that keywords were more than just the function of the Quality Scores to the degree that keywords and overall website performance were effectively interdependent.

Turns out, there is no insider secrets or tricks to gaming the ad placement algorithm. According to Google, the best thing to do to get traffic to your website is to be yourself. "The old advice to college graduates is, 'Do what you love and all else will follow.' In the world of AdWords, the corresponding advice would be, 'Do what's best for your users and your bottom line, and all else will (or at least *should*) follow.'"[67] Just as Coca-Cola discovered in the 1970s, great advertising is still about giving users precisely what they want.

---

66 "Are there swim lanes on the Internet?" B. Pasch. Last Modified March 31, 2014, http://www.brianpasch.com/swim-lanes-Internet/

67 "Settling the (Quality) Score," Google. Last Modified June 24, 2015, http://services.google.com/fh/files/misc/settling-the-quality-score-whitepaper-final.pdf.

CHAPTER 16 SUMMARY

Answer: A, Coca-Cola

Key point: In the final episode of *Mad Men*, Don Draper advertised Coca-Cola and the show aired the company's famous 1971 "Hilltop" commercial. Good marketing back then and today tells the truth in a compelling way. As Google sits as the middleman between brands and consumers, they want brands advertising exactly who they are to connect consumers with relevant results during their searches.

Summary:

- When Acura and Honda analyzed the Google algorithm for ad placement and released guidelines in 2014, Google came out with a white paper that addressed some misconceptions on the same day.
- Rather than using Quality Score, Google uses real-time evaluations of expected CTR, ad relevance, and landing page experience to determine ad placement.
- Instead of a controlled space like a freestyle swim race, Google is more like a shark tank filled with competition from other OEMs, third-party lead providers, and other dealers.
- To stand out, advertisers need to stay true to their brand and manage their overall ad quality.
  - According to Google, advertisers should target for the user's device, make sure their ads and landing pages match the user wants, and invest in coverage on relevant searches in areas where their ads have high relevance.

Seventeen

Selling Cars in the Next Hundred Years

17. Which technology company will produce cars first?

A. Google

B. Uber

C. Facebook

D. Apple

With the rate at which technology changes, the strategies taking people from Car Dogs to Car Dog Millionaires will continue to evolve. The change will come more quickly as yesterday's slow-paced evolution becomes today's quickly synthesized technology revolution. As cars and technology come together in a certain crash course for progress, today's race to car development from an inside out perspective looms large for massive technology companies that sit on the edge of the traditional automotive manufacturing vertical looking for a way into the game.

Apple's electric vehicle and Google's driverless car are in advanced stages of development. After initially setting a 2020 launch date, Apple announced plans to triple the six hundred person team working on their electric car project to push the shipping date up to 2019.[68] With a template from Tesla, at least $70 billion in free cash flow, and a record for building break-through products, the electric vehicle from Apple promises to be evolutionary, if not revolutionary.[69] Remember how the iPhone changed the game?

Tim Cook, Apple President and CEO, indicated that the auto industry is ready for an upheaval in a recent interview with the *Wall Street Journal*. "You see autonomous driving becomes much more important in a huge way in the future," Cook said. "A lot of the major technologies in the car are shifting from today's combustion engine-centric kind of focus, and so it would seem like there will be massive change in that industry."[70]

To make life outside the car and inside the car seamless, Apple released CarPlay—a system that uses audio and touchscreen controls to let drivers use their iPhone capabilities while driving. After Matthew DeBord from Business Insider took CarPlay for a test drive, he raved about the brilliance of using Siri in a car. "It's like having K.I.T.T. or J.A.R.V.I.S. or the computer from 'Star Trek: The Next Generation' installed in your dashboard...Its machine brain understands your human diction. You can actually envision having a relationship with Siri in a car."[71]

---

68 "Apple Targets Electric-Car Shipping Date for 2019," D. Wakabayashi, *Wall Street Journal*, Last Modified September 21, 2015, http://www.wsj.com/articles/apple-speeds-up-electric-car-work-1442857105.

69 "Apple Wants to Start Making Cars as Soon as 2020," T. Higgins, Sydney Morning Herald, Last Modified February 20, 2015, http://www.smh.com.au/business/apple-wants-to-start-making-cars-as-soon-as-2020-20150219-13k4bj.

70 "Tim Cook Talks at WSJDLive About the Future of Cars," *Wall Street Journal* video, 2:30, October 20, 2015, http://www.wsj.com/video/tim-cook-talks-at-wsjdlive-about-the-future-of-cars/65732065-D80B-4A28-B0A1-AC4240FAB7DA.html.

71 "Apple CarPlay Could Completely Disrupt the Auto Industry in One Important Way – And We Tried It," M. DeBord, Business Insider. Last Modified November 22, 2015, http://www.businessinsider.com/apple-carplay-2015-11.

The ability for technology to advance the relationship between machine and man is a profound revelation. While Apple is already making strides toward autonomous control features and electric cars, all indications point to a different path for Google's driverless vehicles. After logging over one million miles on the roads, the Google self-driving project continues to test and improve its hardware and software.[72] Rather than manufacturing the cars, Google hopes to partner with car companies when the technology is ready—hopefully by 2020.[73]

As time goes on and technology progresses, the relationship between media, consumers, and cars will only become increasingly more complex. In the span of our lifetimes, we have witnessed two drastic paradigm shifts unfolding: one in the way we think about cars and the other in the way we buy them.

A toy for the rich in the 1920s, cars came to symbolize independence by the time they reached the mainstream in the 1960s and 1970s.[74] They gave people freedom and control of their lives, as they quite literally put them in the driver's seat. With a car in the garage, people could go wherever they wanted, whenever they wanted.

As more manufacturers joined the market and created different styles of cars, brands relied on advertising strategies to differentiate themselves. As early as the 1950s, classic automotive jingles like Dinah Shore's "See the USA in Your Chevrolet" encouraged

72 "Google's Self-Driving Cars Have Autonomously Driven Over 1 Million Miles," E. Protalinski, *Venture Beat*. Last Modified June 3, 2015, http://venturebeat.com/2015/06/03/googles-self-driving-cars-have-driven-over-1-million-miles/.

73 "Google Inc. Says Self-Driving Car Will Be Ready By 2020," T. Halleck, International Business Times. Last Modified January 14, 2015, http://www.ibtimes.com/google-inc-says-self-driving-car-will-be-ready-2020-1784150.

74 "1913 Ford's Assembly Line Starts Rolling," History, Last Modified (n.d.), Accessed July 28, 2015, http://www.history.com/this-day-in-history/fords-assembly-line-starts-rolling.

consumers to buy.[75] Soon cars were becoming much more than just a means of personal transport—they were an extension of the driver's identity: a space for people to cruise down the road, blast the radio, and feel the wind through their hair. In the good old days, cars represented freedom at the center of everyone's universe.

Today, smartphones have become the declaration of independence for Gen Y and younger, as they represent the gateway to the greater world around us. By using the Internet and apps, we no longer need to rely on cars the way we used to. We can locate the nearest bikes, buses, trains, trolleys, planes, light rails, and subways on our smartphones to find public transportation routes that take us to our destinations. If we choose to drive ourselves, the navigating capabilities of apps like Google Maps on our smartphones far transcend the built-in GPS systems in cars, much less the maps that our parents used to bicker over during Clark Griswold-esque family vacations.

More than just independence, phones represent commerce. To go shopping, we are now picking up our smartphones instead of the car keys to research, browse, and buy products. According to data released by Domo in 2015, Amazon receives 4,310 unique visitors every minute of the day.[76] Other retailers are taking note and making their online stores more appealing to customers. In July 2015, when Amazon announced Prime Day—a blowout sale bigger than Black Friday—competitors Wal-Mart and Best Buy created their own Internet sales days to rival Amazon's deals and shipping discounts.[77]

75 "Dinah Shore 'See the USA in Your Chevrolet,'" YouTube video, Performed by Dinah Shore, Last Modified 2013, https://www.youtube.com/watch?v=boertpyIK0M.

76 "Data Never Sleeps 3.0," Domo.

77 "Walmart Launches Rival Sale to Amazon's Prime Day," H. Malcolm, *USA Today*. Last Modified July 13, 2015, http://www.usatoday.com/story/money/2015/07/13/walmart-sale-against-amazon-prime-day/29973997/.

The overwhelming trend of retailers today moving their stores online means it might not be long before cars, too, can be purchased through websites. Rather than driving people to the dealership, dealers should think in terms of driving the dealership to the people.

Forward-thinking car companies like FIAT have already been dabbling in virtual visits with its FIAT Live Store, which allows customers to connect in real time with FIAT experts who wear virtual-reality headsets in order to give customers an up-close look at the car models in the showroom.[78] This technology bridges the gap between traditional car buying and the future of online shopping. No need to dress-up and drive to the dealership when you can roll out of bed and check things out in the virtual world.

As a result of the evolutionary shift in consumer shopping behavior, dealerships are already facing a significant decline in foot traffic, and quite frankly, car salespeople are getting bored. They spend full days at the dealership just waiting for customers to come in and buy.

THE "UP" BUS

Are you still waiting for the "Up" bus? I recently visited a dealer group just outside of Dallas, Texas, and as I left my meeting I started talking with a green-pea outside the store. The clean-shaven, well-spoken sales consultant had been with the dealership for a few weeks and, via his own account, had only one car out late in November. I asked how the traffic had been, and he indicated that he hadn't seen much of it.

---

78 "Fiat Brazil Brings the Dealership to Your Home with Live Store," R.A. Fera, Fast Company. Last Modified September 17, 2013, http://www.fastcocreate.com/3017584/fiat-brazil-brings-the-dealership-to-your-home-with-live-store.

Then out of the corner of our eyes we noticed a 14-passenger mini bus rolling up. No kidding, the "Up" bus was coming over the horizon, around the corner, and onto the lot. His excitement and interest increased with the possibility on this bright and sunshiny day. No other salespeople were around. This could be HUGE! The fates had—it seemed—intervened to deliver our sales guy with some much needed deals.

However, the only divine intervention that day involved the high school students that exited the bus to continue their church service hours during Thanksgiving week.

The "Up" bus, as you know, is gone.

MEET THE MARKET

Imagine a day when car salespeople create their own schedules. They block time in their calendars to log on from the dealership and do virtual walk-throughs with customers. Gone are the bell-to-bell Saturdays that involve sixteen hour shifts. To accommodate shoppers with day jobs, the salespeople create hours in the evening. If a customer likes a car and decides to buy, their salesperson connects them with a nearby dealership that can demo and deliver it. The transaction is a win-win for both the company and the customer. Car buyers complete all their research remotely and receive a car in record setting times. The salespeople put in the hours that work with their schedule and get paid for their time. Does a workday like this sound too good to be true?

Not to the people already driving for Uber.

UBER'S AMERICAN DREAM

"Make your choice: you can have time off, good money, or good management. Pick any one."

While this familiar car guy saying ruled yesterday's work economy, employment is dramatically changing thanks to break-through companies like Uber. Instead of the traditional nine-to-five job, Uber drivers can choose their hours, make good money, and maintain complete control of their work schedule. Rather than picking either time off, good money, or good management, Uber drivers can pick all three.

In June 2015, just five years after the company's San Francisco launch, Uber had more than one million drivers in their network spanning 311 cities in 58 countries around the world.[79] Today, Uber continues to expand globally as it transforms the transportation industry. To better understand why this employment opportunity is attracting so many drivers, let's get behind the wheel of some of their taxis.

Meet Trisha, an Uber driver who pulls up in Manhattan driving her beige Toyota Sienna minivan. She sports a short brown bob and a thick Brooklyn accent. "I like drivin' for Uber, but all I do in this city is work to pay for everything. New York is so fricken' expensive," she says. Trisha works part time for Uber in addition to a full-time day job to support herself.

"My day job in this city feels like it's controlling me. What are ya thoughts on Pittsburg? I'm debatin' quitting my job and moving there to drive for Uber. The roads are less crowded. I could probably work three or four days a week to live like I do now here," she says. "To me, it's not about money. I don't care

---

79 "Uber: An Oral History," A. Lashinsky, *Fortune*. Last Modified June 3, 2015, http://fortune.com/2015/06/03/uber-an-oral-history/. See also "More Than One Million People Have Now Worked As An Uber Driver," B. Carson, Business Insider. Last Modified June 3, 2015, http://www.businessinsider.com/uber-hits-1-million-drivers-2015-6.

about that really. I just want time to be with my family and to be in control of my life again."

Working for Uber, Trisha recognizes her potential to make good money and still take time off. For other drivers, though, the idea of being their own boss is the most compelling part of driving for the company.

Meet Tony, a forty-something Uber driver from Charleston. He drives full time and makes $90,000 a year. His wife balances spending time at home with the kids and driving part time to bring in $60,000 a year on her own.

"Things are going really great for my family. My wife and I love working for ourselves. It's so liberating to know you can make good money to support your family while working a flexible job," said Tony. "Now I am looking into buying cars for other people and having them drive for Uber as my contractors."

Empowered by the opportunity, Tony is inspired to work even harder to make life better for his family. He can put in overtime, or he can choose to take a day off whenever he wants to be with his family. Call them hustle points, if you will. Lest you remember hustle points came from long hours at the dealership that helped families and careers move ahead.

Today—ironically—as the American dream changes, the companies that offer flexible work schedules are becoming more and more attractive and sought after. The dream no longer involves putting in long hours to convince people to buy things. Selling the car has transformed into driving the car. While the concept behind the work schedule at Uber is novel, it is not an isolated company model. Rather, it's a glimpse of the future workforce. When you can maintain your quality of life, make good money, and take complete control of your schedule, why would you work anywhere else?

BUILDING SUCCESS, ONE LEG AT A TIME

If you want to turn your store into a Car Dog Millionaire dealership, employee happiness is essential. David Rosenberg, CEO of Prime Motor Group in the Boston area, compares running a dealership to owning a three-legged stool. "By three legs, I mean; employee engagement, customer satisfaction, and profitability. Pull out one of those legs and down you go. You can't have one without the other two," Rosenberg said in an interview with Boson.com.[80] Owning 25 stores in the Northeastern US, Rosenberg understands the business and is sharing his knowledge to move the industry forward.

While the analogy of a three-legged stool is one that resonates, what if we could create a more stable chair as a platform to guide our business? If we added just one more leg, we could create a stronger base with better balance. Our four-legged, Car Dog Millionaire approach would build on Rosenberg's theory by adding a supportive leg to help the other three: an online dealership.

An Internet dealership meets customers where they are at, facilitates employee engagement, and enhances profitability through online car sales. By prioritizing digital, you can strengthen the most fundamental parts of your business. Imagine if dealers took on the challenge to develop Internet dealerships, groom their Internet employees, and start thinking about their Internet customers. They would be well on their way to becoming Car Dog Millionaires selling cars online. In fact, some already are.

---

80 "Prime CEO David Rosenberg Grew Up in the Business," P. Kenny, Boston.com. Last Modified March 16, 2015, http://www.boston.com/cars/news-and-reviews/2015/03/16/prime-ceo-david-rosenberg-grew-the-business/bqxlKq3i7Ls4y468FHalfK/story.html.

SELLING CARS ONLINE TODAY

On November 11, 2015, Ali Car (China) set the Guinness World Record for the "Most Cars Sold on a Single Online Platform in 24 Hours," selling 6,506 vehicles during their Single's Day sales.[81] Remember the "World's Greatest Retail Salesman," Joe Girard? It took him *fifteen years* to sell 13,001 cars. China's Alibaba online retail platform sold nearly half as many cars in a single day. If Joe Girard were still selling cars today, you better believe he would be a Car Dog Millionaire and running an Internet dealership—hiring people to build a killer web presence, connecting with customers online, and personally driving over to deliver every car sold.

In the US, one of the top internet automotive retailers today is located in Kellogg, Idaho. That's not a typo—yes, it's in Idaho. Based in a rural town of 2,120 people, Dave Smith Motors uses a competitive pricing strategy and an impressive fleet of 75 online salespeople to attract buyers from across the country.[82] They have a national advertising presence *and* they have a huge purpose. With the Internet, they sell cars across the US and they know how to sell cars online!

As we look toward the future of the automotive industry, it's clear that going digital is the only way through. This is the subtle, yet important nuance in the revised purpose for dealers: Car Dog Millionaires everywhere *will* sell cars online. They will start thinking about how to build their online traffic through quick load

81 "Most Cars Sold on a Single Online Platform in 24 Hours," Guinness World Records. Last Modified November 11, 2015, http://www.guinnessworldrecords.com/.
82 "E-Dealer Pros Sharpen Their Game," M. Gordan, *WardsAuto*. Last Modified April 10, 2012, http://wardsauto.com/wardsauto-e-dealer-100/e-dealer-pros-sharpen-their-game. See also "Geography: Kellogg City, Idaho," United States Census Bureau. Last Modified 2010, http://factfinder.census.gov/faces/tableservices/jsf/pages/productview.xhtml?src=bkmk.

times for pictures, tracking vehicle display pages, and taking the process of closing the deal as close to completely online as humanly possible.

What are you waiting for? Take the models that you see working and guide your dealership team down the path to greater productivity, greater happiness, and better customer experiences. It's time to build your four-legged chair and claim your spot at the table of Car Dog Millionaires.

CHAPTER 17 SUMMARY

Answer: D, Apple

Key Point: Apple will represent the first technology company to *produce* their own vehicle. Google may have driverless cars first, in part because their plans involve developing the technology in concert with existing manufacturers. In true Apple fashion, they seem to be looking to develop their own nameplate and independent operating systems.

Summary:

- The relationship between media, consumers, and cars will become increasingly more complex over time.
- Significant paradigm shifts are already occurring:
  - Cars used to represent freedom at the center of everyone's universe; now smartphones have become the portal for independence, commerce, and freedom in our society.
  - Internet departments are now being replaced by Internet dealerships.
- Companies in general and dealerships in particular will provide "purpose" to employees alongside flexibility and independence in work schedules in the future.
- A four-legged, Car Dog Millionaire approach to Rosenberg's three-legged theory would feature the following four aspects as the most vital components to a dealership's success: customer satisfaction, employee engagement, profitability, and a digital dealership.
- Car Dog Millionaires of the future *will* sell cars online!

Part 2

Digital Dealer Dialogues

Dealer Dialogue Introduction

Bill Bradley's 1976 book, *Life on the Run,* helped guide my thinking for what to share in this book. Much of what brought these chapters to life involves conversations with dealers. Snippets of these conversations appear earlier in the book. However, some of the conversations were better served in their own section.

As a backdrop, this interview along with the following chapters identify how conversations can and do change behavior. What Bradley tried to do in *Life on the Run:* "[W]as to allow people to hear, feel and see what it was like to be a professional basketball player crisscrossing America for eight months a year, playing sometimes as many as a hundred and twenty games in a single season...I had wanted to avoid idealizing the life."[83]

Bradley was a classmate of my father who, I believe, showed great discipline in handing the book over to me circa 1978 (when I was in third grade). As I crisscross America today spreading the good word for automotive digital marketing, I can still remember reading the opening chapter. Somehow it seared into my brain as I read it over and over again as only an eight-year-old would remember.

"Hey, man, when you gonna guard me?"

---

83 Bradley, Bill. *Life on the Run.* New York: Quadrangle/New York Times Book, 1976.

"What's the matter, too old?"

"You just one no-playin' white motherf**ker."

"I ain't even the doctor and I'm operatin' all over you."[84]

The spoken word becomes exponentially powerful in a written format. It's from that place that I share my experiences throughout the years with the various dealers I've worked with in order to support their business.

Bradley, competitor and athlete that he was, washes off the trash talk and helps the Knicks mount a furious comeback to open the story. With eight seconds left, the Knicks are down by one and he's fouled, which sends him to the free-throw line for two free throws. Despite the hot streak that brought him to the moment, Bradley can't help but remember all his failures during the first three quarters of the game. He's on fire but misses the first free throw.

Well, at least there's a second free throw to tie the game, he reminds himself. Bradley dribbles three times, hurls the basketball twenty feet over the backboard, and starts to laugh, laugh, laugh...

Whether you think the sequence is a dream or an actual experience, you have to take Bradley at face value. Of all his intellectual, athletic, and communicative abilities, he can't believe the world hangs on to the one that allows him to play basketball at a high level. The part of the game and process that's motivating and interesting to him is the conversation and the possibility of it all.

With that as a backdrop, I share with you some of the conversations with my dealer partners. I hope you find the following entertaining and accurate, and never underestimate the power of the conversation as motivation to drive you to the place where Car Dog Millionaires live.

---

84 Ibid.

Eighteen

Welcome, Mr. Dealer

Politics aside, the fist bump heard around the world occurred when Michelle Obama knocked knuckles with her husband as he claimed the 2008 Democratic nomination.[85] To date, the fist bump and the high five have been celebratory signature moves.

In the car industry, business still happens over handshakes. Whether used to greet someone or seal a deal, a firm handshake shows mutual respect. A weak handshake, on the other hand, can stop commerce even before it gets started. No matter how you cut it, the context of the contact you make is important. Well… unless it doesn't happen. Then you may have a different problem altogether.

In this case, it turns out that this general manager had a little something he wanted to share, too. He hated everything about what I represented.

JIM: *Hi, I'm Jim. It's good to meet you. [Hand extends for handshake.]*
DEALER: *[Hand stays in pocket.] It's guys like you that screwed up the business.*

---

85 "A Brief History of the Fist Bump." M. Stephey, *Time.* Last Modified June 5, 2008, http://content.time.com/time/nation/article/0,8599,1812102,00.html

JIM: *Sir?*

DEALER: *You "Internet gurus."*

JIM: *Oh, that. I had nothing to do with that. Al Gore deserves all the credit. [Chuckles in attempt to laugh it off.]*

DEALER: *No, I'm serious. It's BS. I don't see why you couldn't just leave well enough alone. It was bad enough you let people see the invoice on new cars, but now you give them the lowest prices on used cars.*

JIM: *Wait a second...*

DEALER: *Hold on. I'm not done. You'll get your turn. That's why I hired you. I just gotta say this.*

DEALER: *We used to make money—I mean, real money. If you knew your cars and knew what they were worth, it was a good business. Nowadays I spend all this time trying to get people in the store, and you know who I hate more than you?*

JIM: *I'm the Internet, right?*

DEALER: *Damn right, you're the Internet. I hate AutoTrader more than you. How I pay them $5,000 a month to advertise my cars. My cars. My f***ing cars. And then I see how cheap I can sell them. I don't know why I'm in this business anymore. Really...how you are going to help me? You're just another f***ing vendor who's going to extract money out my pocket and I honestly won't know what the f*** you've done at the end. I'm actually the one who's selling the cars.*

JIM: *Actually, that's what I want to talk to you about. You've got some problems.*

DEALER: *You don't think I don't know that I have problems?*

JIM: *Well, first you should stop advertising.*

DEALER: *This is f'ng beautiful. The Internet guru is here to tell me not to spend money. Pray tell?*

JIM: *Of the 120 cars you have on ground, 90 of them haven't had a price change in the last seven days. Nobody's watching the shop. At the beginning you said knowing your cars was key. That part hasn't changed.*

DEALER: *Mr. Internet, I will tell YOU we don't need to lower our prices. We need to make money. Once we get them in, we set the price and people can buy what we got at that price or not. I don't give a good damn.*

JIM: *I didn't say lower price; I said reprice. You should actually raise prices when the cheapest cars in the market sell. I guarantee you are leaving money on the table. Guarantee it 100 percent.*

DEALER: *How can you guarantee it?*

JIM: *Because I've looked at your inventory and the world changes more in ninety days than the prices on your website.*

DEALER: *I f***ing hate the Internet.*

Nineteen

Home of the Free
and the Brave

After a few weeks of working with one of my dealers to strengthen his marketing, he gave me a call and a decent piece of his mind. Sure he was selling more cars, but he was sick of spending more money. The last quarter he failed to make a profit. Did I understand that? He needed to meet with his team and requested my presence the following day. I complied, bracing myself for the worst: a stubborn dealer who sounded ready to show me the door.

> DEALER: *Jim, we brought you in today to let you know that we are NOT going to fire you.*
> JIM: *Are NOT?*
> DEALER: *That's right, we are NOT going to fire you, but you are going to have to get more involved.*
> JIM: *Yes, sir.*
> DEALER: *We need to do something differently, and to be real honest, my team said that you weren't the thing we needed to do differently. I thought it might be. I even had*

one of my guys say he should be fired before you guys should be. He's been with me for ten years.

JIM: *Wow.*

DEALER: *But here's the deal: I need you to do something that doesn't cost anything. My digital spending is exploding, and the website traffic is there, but they aren't buying.*

JIM: *So you want something for free?*

DEALER: *Yes. Yes, I do. Best things in life are free, or so I hear. I wouldn't personally know.*

JIM: *I have something.*

DEALER: *Really? I thought you'd go back and serve up some ideas.*

JIM: *No, sir. I'll pull the info up right now. You are getting killed on speed.*

DEALER: *I don't know what you are trying to imply, but none of my employees are on drugs, Jim. However, if they were going to be on one drug, I suppose "speed" would be preferable.*

JIM: *Sir, I think you meant that to be funny, and under normal circumstances I would find that humorous. However, you started by saying that you were considering letting me go.*

DEALER: *Aw, Jim. Don't take it personal. I just thought we might need to shake things up a bit. My team really likes your team.*

JIM: *Yes, sir. Back to the speed thing. What's the most important stat at the NFL Combine?*

DEALER: *I'm sure it's speed. Do you think those guys are on speed? Hah! Who knows what they are on.*

JIM: *Tenths of a second in forty-yard dash time can translate into millions of dollars. Same holds true for you. You can't teach speed, and it becomes even more important at elite levels. The difference between a ninety miles per hour fastball and one going a hundred miles per hour is the difference between a Hall of Fame career and the minor leagues. That's what we're taking about for you.*

DEALER: *I thought I heard you say "free."*

JIM: *Yes sir, we're on same page. So Google just started sharing something with web developers that measures your web speed, and it's FREE. It's the Google Developers PageSpeed Insights tool, and your website scores 50 out of 100 on the mobile side and 63 out of 100 on the desktop side.*

DEALER: *That's horrible. Jesus, I need to fire my Internet director, don't I?*

JIM: *No one needs to be fired.*

DEALER: *Those scores are horrible. Holy cow, why didn't you tell me about this? I should fire you for making me drag this out of you.*

JIM: *Google released this tool last month. No one knows about it. You are the first dealer I've shared it with. The first and only to date.*

DEALER: *How's it free?*

JIM: *You already pay your Internet service provider more than a $1,000 a month to take care of your website. This Google developer's tool tells them where they need to tweak things to make your site run faster. It's like the diagnostic tools on your service drive. You don't necessarily* know the codes or how to fix the equipment, but your technicians do.

DEALER: *OK, I just pulled up Google's tool, but I don't really get it. It says I should "Eliminate render-blocking JavaScript and CSS in above-the-fold-content." This is way over my head.*

JIM: *That's OK. Look right below where it says "Show How to Fix." When you click on that, it gives the information to your website team on how they can fix it. Same deal as the technician. All you have to do is keep track of the score at an executive level.*

DEALER: *Jim, this seems like BS.*

JIM: *It's from Google.*

DEALER: *Not buying it.*

JIM: *I'll personally guarantee it.*

DEALER: *How?*

JIM: *You get the score on these to 80 via your Internet service provider on mobile AND desktop by the end of this quarter, and I'll guarantee that your free website traffic grows by 10 percent quarter over quarter.*

DEALER: *What's that mean?*

JIM: *Hold your ISP accountable. Your marketing manager can do this by sending weekly updates to you. When you feel like you aren't getting traction, call them. Do what you're doing with me. Tune them up. Get to 80, and then we'll be moving closer to full speed.*

DEALER: *Why not 100?*

JIM: *I think everyone will give up if you set the bar that high. Eighty is achievable and puts you ahead of ALL your competitors in your market.*

Chapter 19

DEALER: *I don't even know why this matters.*

JIM: *From the consumer side, if a website takes a long time to load, we leave. Sometimes even before the site loads. Google is now being transparent about what they are tracking. Relevance and speed have always mattered, but for the first time they are giving you insight on how to get faster.*

DEALER: *So?*

JIM: *It's the difference between you or your competition showing up. Right now your competition is faster than you, so Google will give them the benefit of the doubt. Your competitors are getting more of the free visibility.*

DEALER: *This is all so much BS.*

JIM: *Right now you are getting about 1,000 visitors a day to your website, and you have a Moneyball Factor of 1 percent. Add 10 percent more traffic a day at no additional cost, keep your Moneyball Factor the same, and you WILL SELL thirty more car deals this month.*

DEALER: *I knew there was a reason why my team likes you guys. Oh, but you know I'm going to hold YOU to the guarantee.*

JIM: *Or I get fired?*

DEALER: *Yes, exactly. Let's go to lunch.*

Twenty

That Viral Sensation

DEALER: *Jim, I want you to come up with something for me that will go viral.*

JIM: *That's not really what we do.*

DEALER: *You're a digital marketing agency, right?*

JIM: *Yes.*

DEALER: *You do YouTube, right?*

JIM: *Yes.*

DEALER: *You've had me in your studio and we make commercials, right?*

JIM: *Yes.*

DEALER: *Well, then let's just film something that goes viral. I just think this is going to be a great partnership. You're going to be able to tell people about how you helped us grow our business, and a viral video seems to me like it would be perfect for you and me to help get us on the map.*

JIM: *This is why I wanted to invite you to lunch today.*

DEALER: *What?*

JIM: *I think your guys are spending too much time waiting for the big idea and the big gross deals when what they should be doing is holding their teams accountable for daily performance goals.*

DEALER: *Give me what you mean.*

JIM: *I went over a sales tracking worksheet with your GSM, and he doesn't track leads and closing ratios on a weekly basis. He tracks them monthly. I'm trying to be respectful, but that's not really tracking. Your service director wants to do a wholesale parts site.*

Viral videos are distractions. They are bright shiny stars that you never really touch. You dream about them because you see them, but it doesn't help business. I'd be more inclined to believe that we'd still be working together in a year if your team focused on the sales operations metrics that I talked with them about.

DEALER: *That's not what agencies do.*

JIM: *We are a digital sales operations company. If you want to catch lightning in a bottle, I can help you do that, but it won't help you sell cars. It MAY get you notoriety, but in today's twenty-four-hour news cycle, notoriety is highly correlated with controversy.*

DEALER: *Well, I don't want to do anything controversial.*

JIM: *Then you really don't want to have something go viral.*

DEALER: *It does NOT have to be controversial to go viral.*

JIM: *Agreed. Here are your other options. You have to have music. Or a guy doing the history of dance in five minutes. Or a sneezing baby panda. Or the Harlem Shake. None of those will help you sell cars and really don't connect to dealership life.*

DEALER: *What is the Harlem Shake? Whatever.*

JIM: *The best we could hope for is to take video of the demolition of your facility and hope that something exciting happens.*

DEALER: *I want the community to get excited about the new building, not the demolition of the old one.*

JIM: *I mean this so respectfully, but this conversation— while engaging—isn't forwarding our efforts to help you sell more cars.*

DEALER: *But this is what ad agencies do.*

JIM: *Yeah, I think the Internet changed everything. We are in a different place today.*

DEALER: *Come on, I'll pay $5,000 and you come up with something.*

JIM: *I would have someone hit golf balls through car windows or, geez, I don't know, but I know these things don't help sell cars. You have a great name in the community. Maybe this is more about a need to be seen differently in the community. Help me understand where you want to go.*

DEALER: *I was thinking something like taking the video from the high school football game where we put a truck on the field on Friday night.*

JIM: *Well, that won't go viral, but with $5,000 we can get 50,000 views.*

DEALER: *I guess that could work.*

JIM: *It wouldn't be viral like Beyoncé falling down the stairs at a concert. That's viral.*

DEALER: *What would it cost to get a million views?*

JIM: *$100,000*

DEALER: *That's a lot.*

JIM: *$8,000 a month.*

Chapter 20

DEALER: *How many views does Beyoncé have?*

JIM: *Around 7.2 million. Over seven years, though.*

DEALER: *That's what I want: a million a year.*

JIM: *The video doesn't really help Beyoncé sell records, for that matter.*

DEALER: *Beyoncé is already on the map. I just want to be on the map.*

JIM: *Then let's sell some cars and get your sales teams off the idea. Do you remember the dragon tamer (see Chapter 14) who spent too much time on marketing?*

DEALER: *Oh yeah...the sales guy who focused too much energy on marketing and not enough on selling cars. All right, all right, I get it. So if we don't need a viral campaign, what do we need?*

JIM: *You need to figure out how to solve your marketing puzzle.*

DEALER: *Right, so tell me how to do that.*

JIM: *It's going to be a bit of a complicated process—do you know how to solve a Rubik's Cube?*

DEALER: *No...what does that have to do with selling cars?*

JIM: *Everything. There are over forty-three quintillion combinations and only one is right for your make, your model, and your market each and every month.*

Twenty One

Of Course, I Own My Name!
Right? I Do. Don't I?

Dateline:
8:45 a.m.
Saturday Morning
Anywhere, USA

DEALER: *I don't show up on my listing when I Google my name.*
JIM: *At ALL?*
DEALER: *At all!*
JIM: *Where are you?*
DEALER: *I'm @ the DEALER:ship.*
JIM: *No. Which search engine.*
DEALER: *Internet Explorer.*
JIM: *What? No. Search engine. Like Google, Yahoo, Bing?*
DEALER: *Google.*
JIM: *I typed in your name and I see our ad, plus you are number one.*
DEALER: *Well, yeah, I see that.*

Chapter 21

JIM: *That's a lot different than, "Not at all."*

DEALER: *Not really. You told me the goal was to own your name. You said to own Google Page One. I wanted to own Google.*

JIM: *You'd have to buy stock if you want to own Google.*

DEALER: *What? I just want to own my name.*

JIM: *You do.*

DEALER: *We suck.*

JIM: *So you have AutoTrader and CarGurus in your paid click space. You know what you don't have in the organic space for your name?*

DEALER: *What?*

JIM: *Social media*

DEALER: *Not related.*

JIM: *Oh, but it is.*

DEALER: *Don't want to hear it. I purposefully didn't sign up for that with you, and I post things from time to time, so I really don't want to hear it. I just had a post at the auto show that was good.*

JIM: *That was a month ago on Twitter. There's been nothing since.*

DEALER: *So?*

JIM: *So Twitter is on page two of Google.*

DEALER: *So?*

JIM: *You want to own page one. If you let us or even have someone at the store get active for you on Twitter, we will move one of your competitors or third-party lead providers OFF the page for your name. We will also be controlling the message.*

DEALER: *What?*

JIM: *Wow. You haven't posted on Facebook since October of last year.*

DEALER: *So.*

JIM: *Facebook is ranked number eleven, just off page one. So if we were get active and start posting more frequently with meaningful, engaging content, then we'd move up and one of your competitors would go down to page two, where they would effectively be irrelevant.*

DEALER: *Yeah, that's right. I remember you told me one time that page two on Google was "irrelevant." So now you are trying to sell me a social media package, and all of sudden all this social media stuff on page two becomes "relevant"?*

JIM: *I couldn't care less if you buy, but if you want to solve your problem, you better grab the low-hanging fruit. It's dealer's choice.*

DEALER: *If I do nothing?*

JIM: *Competitors stay there. Third-party lead providers seize the opening and sell leads back to you.*

DEALER: *If I post?*

JIM: *You can post, but I'd think you'd be better off running a dealership. Plus, you can't find a dedicated employee who knows your business and cares as much as we do for the price you're paying us.*

DEALER: *I still think I want to do this myself.*

JIM: *Then you HAVE to do it.*

DEALER: *I do some stuff.*

JIM: *Not enough to get you onto Google Page One, and you are blowing me up on Saturday.*

DEALER: *I do pay per click with you.*

JIM: *Yes, and it's working. You are taking up the number-one spot with your sponsored ads.*

DEALER: *I just don't want to do social.*

JIM: *Here's the deal. Do you want to NOT do social more than you want your competitors to show up on Google Page One for your name?*

DEALER: *It's a waste of money.*

JIM: *Because it doesn't sell you cars, right?*

DEALER: *RIGHT!*

JIM: *It's keeping you from selling cars, though.*

DEALER: *How?*

JIM: *Because each click a competitor gets off your name is one less opportunity you have to do business.*

DEALER: *What do you thinks it's worth?*

JIM: *Each missed click? Gosh, I don't know...wait, I do know. So we pay Google about $1 per click and they are among all nine other listings on the remaining pages generating an average of several thousand clicks.*

More specifically, you get 12,000 visitors per month. About half come from your name. So it's safe to say that, spread among all your competitors, you are leaking around 5,000 clicks a month that you wouldn't lose if you had Facebook and Twitter up a few spots higher up in the Google Page One Ranking for your name.

DEALER: *So $1 a click...are you going to charge me $5,000?*

JIM: *No. Less than a third of that.*

DEALER: *I still don't like it.*

JIM: *I don't like it either. It does make sense, though.*

DEALER: *Yeah. I think I'm going to just do this on my own for a while so I can learn it.*

JIM: *Sir, you are the partner in a huge dealership and you are going to manage your own social media page that would cost you less than a $1,000 a month so you can say what? "That I manage my own social media page." Other general managers would laugh at you.*

DEALER: *I don't like social media.*

JIM: *So why in the hell would you manage it?*

DEALER: *Still don't like it.*

JIM: *Google doesn't care. Facebook doesn't care. More importantly, customers don't care.*

JIM: *Look, Mr. Dealer, I've known you to be a good businessman through the years, but you're letting your anxiety and need to control drive this. And with all due respect, it's affecting your business. Being a good read of people is one thing, but being a good read of your financials is another. This is the heart of digital sales operations, and you are not reading what the numbers are telling you.*

DEALER: *I'll sign the deal if you guarantee I'll be on Google Page One in thirty days.*

JIM: *Give me ninety, and I'll guarantee it.*

DEALER: *Done. Thanks, Jim.*

Twenty Two

Throwing It All Away

If you don't recognize the value of your website, you might as well just throw your advertising money into the ocean—like this next dealer was about to do.

> DEALER: *I have a brand-new dealership. Brand-new. How much should I spend on advertising?*
> JIM: *Well, let's talk about that.*
> DEALER: *Yeah, I have a dealership in another market, but this is an open point. I think I should spend about $50,000 to get it going.*
> JIM: *Well, how many cars do you want to sell?*
> DEALER: *Say 150?*
> JIM: *New? And used?*
> DEALER: *Yes.*
> JIM: *How many are you selling today?*
> DEALER: *About 70.*
> JIM: *So help me understand how you came up with $50,000?*
> DEALER: *I figured $300 cost per sale would put me at $45,000 to $50,000. I need to grow the business. Plus, since it's a new point, I am getting my supplemental*

vehicle allocation from the factory. Actually, I AM going to grow the business.

JIM: *So how many salespeople do you have?*

DEALER: *Seven.*

JIM: *Whoa!*

DEALER: *What?*

JIM: *You're about to pay for a vacation to Bermuda.*

DEALER: *Why Bermuda?*

JIM: *I call it the Automotive Bermuda Triangle. It's when you'd be better off paying for a trip to Bermuda than you would be spending your money with me. With seven guys you should expect to sell seventy cars...*

DEALER: *I think my guys can do twenty each.*

JIM: *Since this is a new dealership, have any of these guys been with you for more than thirty days?*

DEALER: *No...*

JIM: *So NADA says 8.5 cars per salesperson on national average. Let's say you're above average by 15 percent and we'll use ten cars per person. Still, that only pencils to seventy cars.*

DEALER: *Well, I have 120 units on ground this month to sell, and new product will be arriving in July. I want to be ready and make a splash! Plus, we have $2,000 worth of F150 conquest cash.*

JIM: *Make a splash, save some cash, and use some of that $50,000 to bring more salespeople on board. Without it, you'll bring in traffic and then wonder why it didn't turn into sales. Right now, you don't have enough salespeople or inventory to sell 150 cars. Don't spend the money with me. I won't take it.*

DEALER: *But I have 120 cars! New and used.*

JIM: *So let's say you turned your inventory one time: you'd sell 120. Tell me how you can sell 150. Do you have a huge arrival soon?*

DEALER: *I told you that's in July. We should be getting 120 more on top of the 120 base, then.*

JIM: *Well, if you keep your days' supply around forty-five days, you'd be good to go in July.*

DEALER: *I sell some units faster. I don't keep used cars more than sixty days. I just want to be ready to go today. Are you saying you won't help me?*

JIM: *I'm saying that I AM helping you.*

DEALER: *What?*

JIM: *You will sell 150 cars in July. That's why you should spend the money in July, NOT June. It's June 3, to be exact, and you have seven salespeople. If you spend $50,000 in June, you'd be wasting every penny. You don't have the units. You don't have the people. And without them, you're stuck in the middle of the Automotive Bermuda Triangle.*

DEALER: *So to get out, I need more people, inventory... and what's the third part? Money?*

JIM: *The cost per sale you were talking about earlier IS important. But I look at website visitors and your Moneyball Factor.*

DEALER: *OK!*

JIM: *It's your truest closing ratio. If you can determine how many visitors come to your website versus how many cars you sold, we can know how to get to where you want to be.*

DEALER: *How so?*

JIM: *So let's say you have around 7,500 people who come to your website and you have a 1 percent Moneyball Factor. That's seventy-five car sales. That's where you probably are today.*

DEALER: *I'm tracking. I'm tracking.*

JIM: *Well, if you have the people and inventory, then we can spend the advertising dollars to get you 10,000 visitors to your website. If we maintain your closing ratio of 1 percent, we then sell...?*

DEALER: *One hundred units. So if I want to sell 150 cars based on 1 percent Moneyball Factor...*

JIM: *Then we get you to 15,000 visitors.*

DEALER: *Double my visitors.*

JIM: *And keep your Moneyball Factor intact.*

DEALER: *How much will that cost me?*

JIM: *A lot less than $50,000.*

DEALER: *So spend nothing today?*

JIM: *Go hire some people. Please.*

DEALER: *On it. I like this. That's good stuff, man. I will call you.*

Twenty Three

An Inventory Shock

In March 2011, an earthquake triggered a powerful tsunami—now known as the Tohoku earthquake. At 2:46 p.m., a 9.0 magnitude earthquake took place 231 miles northeast of Tokyo, Japan, at a depth of 15.2 miles. As the fourth most powerful earthquake measured since 1900, it claimed many lives, created billions in loss, and halted production at most Japanese companies.

While sales spiked for Chevrolet and Ford products, Toyota and Honda products became less if not completely unavailable. Dealers who had a plan minimized damage. Those who did not woke up to a wicked hangover a few months later that helped the domestics reclaim market share majority for the first time in several years.

Dateline, March 12: One day after Tsunami.

> DEALER: *Thanks for sitting down with me. You said you wanted to go over this days' supply deal. Seemed real urgent.*
> JIM: *Yeah, it's a now thing for sure.*
> DEALER: *So what's the deal?*
> JIM: *Let's be direct. So how many cars do you have on the ground from Japan?*

DEALER: *About 200.*

JIM: *And how many of those will you sell this month?*

DEALER: *Hold on. Here: 125 this month.*

JIM: *So you have a forty-five to fifty days' supply. Let's check that. Yes, calculator shows forty-eight days.*

DEALER: *What's the point?*

JIM: *Your OEM isn't going to be able to build replacement vehicles. Your volume has to go down and your grosses have to go up. You have to treat your customers better.*

DEALER: *Hey, we treat customers just fine.*

JIM: *Sure, but do you treat them Lexus better?*

DEALER: *No.*

JIM: *Lexus better is the new goal.*

DEALER: *Why?*

JIM: *So if you sell at your current pace, you will be out of vehicles on or about May 1.*

DEALER: *Don't see it. My number this month is 125.*

JIM: *That's your factory number for March, but the factory got hit by a tsunami that destroyed Japan. Seven nuclear plants are down. The factory is not going to be back up anytime soon.*

DEALER: *So let's say you are right—what can I do about it anyway? I'm just here trying to sell cars every day.*

JIM: *First, slow down with your sales guys.*

DEALER: *They need a kick in the @$$. We should be do-ing 250 out of this store.*

JIM: *Not now. Not this quarter. Probably not next. This changes your management style. You have to hold for gross.*

DEALER: *This is BS.*

JIM: *Making money and keeping your employees is BS?*

DEALER: *No. Just that a godforsaken tsunami in Japan is making me change my entire business model.*

JIM: *Well, it's only a problem if it's a problem. Some of the other general managers in town will miss this.*

DEALER: *What if you are wrong?*

JIM: *I'm not. If you slow down your turn rate and make more gross profit per unit, you will thank me in June. Guys will be dying and you will be able to set the market.*

DEALER: *How do you know the plants are down?*

JIM: *It's the fourth largest earthquake of all time. Have you seen the pictures?*

DEALER: *So?*

JIM: *Plus, Japanese companies and people don't discuss shameful things openly. It's shameful to have your business to be unsightly, much less be unproductive. It's not their fault, but the plants are down for the foreseeable future. The Japanese will work like crazy to fix everything, but they won't be open about the progress they are or aren't making. One day they will announce they are back and running, and that will be that.*

DEALER: *So how much gross per unit should I make?*

JIM: *Well, let's figure it out. If the plant is down for one month, then you need to sell how many cars at how much per copy?*

DEALER: *You make it sound like one of those stupid math problems from high school. You know the one where one train leaves Boston going 70 mph and one train leaves Dallas going 100 mph. Where do they hit?*

JIM: *Where do they hit?*

DEALER: *I don't where, but I know it's going to be one helluva an explosion!*

JIM: *You're funny. OK, so if you were getting backfilled inventory, you'd make $1,500 a copy. So on 125 units, you would make $187,500 for three months or $562,500. If you have only 200 units for the same three months you would need to make $2,800 a copy...$2,812 to be exact.*

DEALER: *Nearly twice as much. This business is crazy. Not only do we have to stop sales, but we have service recalls. And now we have an ever-living, mother-loving tsunami. I just don't know why I stay in this business.*

JIM: *You love it. And at $2,800 a copy, you better show some love to your customers. Hence, the need for Lexus-like customer service. VIP treatment. VIP appointments. VIP trade appraisals. You are going to need to take trades like crazy. It's doable, but you will have to set gross bonuses instead of volume bonuses with the sales team.*

DEALER: *How do I know the others in the market will do this?*

JIM: *They won't AND that's OK. It's going to hurt more at first for you because the other dealers don't know what you know. But you already know it's like a haircut. You can't add inventory once it's gone. The other dealers will keep selling the only precious vehicles they have or that they will get until June, July, or August. Either way, you will own the market if you slow down today. You will make it up in gross AND volume if you play this right.*

DEALER: *I didn't get to where I am by tapping the breaks on anything. Not ever. Not once. This is a "now" business. I have to sell cars today. I can't explain this to the owner.*

JIM: *You can't NOT explain this to the owner. Take the challenge to be the number-one gross dealer this month. It's not that you want to, but you have to, AND it will pay huge dividends. Your owner will love you for this.*

DEALER: *You seem so sure of this. So let's say I don't change. What happens then?*

JIM: *You run $1,500 a copy and run out of cars on May 1. You make $300,000 gross.*

DEALER: *So if I make $300,000 gross by May 1, I'm good. That works. End of story.*

JIM: *No, sir. Then your salespeople quit because they have nothing to sell in May and you also have effectively killed June and July. March and April will be OK, but your salespeople will starve during the summer months or at least until the OEM gets back to building cars.*

DEALER: *What if I just ran $2,000 a copy. When would I run out?*

JIM: *Can't say, but you should make it well into May.*

DEALER: *$2,500 a copy.*

JIM: *June.*

DEALER: *This better work.*

JIM: *It will work.*

It did work. The dealer slowed in March while maintaining inventory, sales personnel, and better customer satisfaction. On April 20, 2011, nearly a month after the tsunami, Toyota announced drastic production cuts. Toyota stopped production altogether between the dates of April 28 to May 9, 2011.[86] Full production returned later that year, with some industry experts believing production implications were still being felt as far out as December 2011.[87]

---

86 "Toyota Making Drastic Production Cuts after Japan Quake, Tsunami," CNN Wire Staff. Last Modified April 20, 2011, http://www.cnn.com/2011/WORLD/asiapcf/04/20/japan.toyota/.

87 "Toyota One Year after the Tsunami," M. Batenchuk, Be Car Chic. Last Modified March 12, 2012, http://becarchic.com/2012/03/12/industry-pulse-toyota-one-year-after-the-tsunami/.

About the Authors

Jim Flint grows businesses—his, yours, and almost anything else he seems to touch. Jim's digital marketing agency, Local Search Group, received recognition as the fastest growing advertising and marketing firm in Texas. With 4,213 percent revenue growth, *Inc. Magazine* also named Local Search Group the sixty-fifth-fastest growing company in the entire United States. Prior to founding Local Search Group, Flint developed sales plans, financial plans, and marketing strategies for companies, including Nike, Toyota, and multifranchise dealer groups. As a twenty-year industry veteran, Jim is widely recognized as a thought leader in digital sales operations, marketing, and advertising.

Michelle Lenzen is a graduate of the University of Illinois, where she earned her degree in advertising. A freelance writer, certified teacher, and professional online marketer, she also studied comedy at the Second City in Chicago and lends her skills to making boring business stuff more entertaining in *Car Dog Millionaire*, her debut book cowritten with Jim Flint.

CPSIA information can be obtained at www.ICGtesting.com
Printed in the USA
LVOW06*2238080116

469292LV00002B/2/P

9 780692 596432